CLASSIC ◆ GUITARS

A PRIMER FOR THE VINTAGE GUITAR COLLECTOR

OVER 125 BRAND NAMES DESCRIBED, GUITAR TERMINOLOGY, PARTS INFORMATION,
HOW TO RECOGNIZE COUNTERFEITS & FORGERIES, OVER 540 PHOTOGRAPHS

BY WILLIE G. MOSELEY

FOREWORD BY STAN JAY

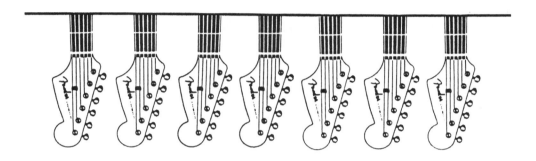

FRONT COVER PHOTOS BY STAN JAY
TOP:
Guild Mark 7-a unique deep body, double cutaway jazz guitar
made for a trade show in the mid-1960s
Gretsch Monkees Model guitar
Gibson 1954 Les Paul Standard, "Gold Top" #4 2978

BOTTOM:
Martin 1936 000-28 herringbone - a very rare guitar
Fender May 1962 Precision Bass, sunburst
1941 Gibson L-5P Premiere (the first model cutaway Gibson archtop)
and 1948 Gibson L-5P Premiere

BACK COVER PHOTOS BY STAN JAY
TOP:
1968 Martin Brazilian rosewood D-45, (1 of 230 made)
Lefty Fernandes Stratocaster copy
Vilette Citron electric solid body guitar - started in 1979 and finished by
Harvey Citron in 1991

BOTTOM:
Benedetto Cremona, cutaway jazz guitar, brown
Gibson 1958 Flying V #8 2691 Most mint condition example in the world
National Style 0 metal body guitar

Typesetting by Angela Marchionno
Pasteup by Shelby Middlebrook
Layout and Production by Ron Middlebrook

Library of Congress Catalog Card Number
91-70519

SAN 683-8022
ISBN 0-931759-52-8

batrm

ACKNOWLEDGMENTS

What began as a fleeting bit of wishful thinking ultimately ended up in my spending hours in the office, pecking away at the Smith Corona (you ought to see the amount spent on typewriter ribbons, correction fluid, etc.!), not to mention hours spent on the phone, talking long distance with manufacturers, vintage shops and guitar buffs. Nevertheless, my preliminary informal survey had indicated that there is a need for a book such as this, so I feel the effort was well spent.

I would like to thank the following manufacturers, vintage dealers and individuals for their active input and encouragement:

Fender Musical Instruments (Bill Carson & Mike Caroff)
Gibson U.S.A. (Tim Shaw)
Kramer Music Products (Jon Hoenge)
Rickenbacker (Rachel Leathers & Theresa Cleaver)
Ovation/Kaman (Nancy Heacox & John Budny)
Alembic (Cathy Nelson)
Sears (Dan McGee)
George Gruhn (Gruhn Guitars, Nashville, TN)
Matt Umanov (Matt Umanov Guitars, New York City)
Marc Silber (Reich-Silber Museum, Berkley, CA)
Mandolin Brothers, Staten Island, NY (Stan Jay & Larry Wexer)
Michael Holmes (New Bedford, MA)
Skip Henderson (City Lights Music, New Brunswick, NJ)
Cleo & Al Greenwood (Vintage Guitar Magazine)
Tom Wheeler
Tut Campbell (Dixie Guitars, Smyrna, GA)
Don Schwartz (Music Trader, Panama City, FL)
Bob Hartman (Maurer & Co., Schaumberg, IL)
Richard Smith (Fullerton, CA)
James Werner (Letts, IA)

Most of all I'd like to thank Gail and Elizabeth for their patience and understanding. I love you both so very much.

FOR HONEY

The piano lessons didn't work out,
but she always encouraged my writing ventures

ABOUT THE AUTHOR:
Willie G. Moseley, a self-described "aging rock & roller", is a feature writer and columnist for Vintage Guitar magazine. He resides in Montgomery, Alabama with his wife Gail, daughter Elizabeth and their pet Dachshund, "Motorhead".

Moseley's next book project is an anthology of his articles and columns from Vintage Guitar.

I WOULD LIKE TO THANK THE FOLLOWING INDIVIDUALS AND BUSINESSES FOR ALLOWING ME TO PHOTOGRAPH THEIR INSTRUMENTS:

AAA PAWN: PENSACOLA, FL
A & D MERCHANDISE MART: PENSACOLA, FL
A.J.'S GUITAR & SOUND: CLANTON, AL
ACME SALES CO.: ANNISTON, AL
ADAMS PAWN SHOP: PENSACOLA, FL
AL'S GUN & PAWN: PACE, FL
ALBANY MUSIC & PAWN: ALBANY, GA
ALPINE PAWN SHOP: COLUMBUS, GA
RICHARD ALEXANDER: DOTHAN, AL
ANDERSON'S PAWN: DALEVILLE, AL
ART'S MUSIC SHOP: MONTGOMERY, AL
ART'S MUSIC SHOP: DOTHAN, AL
ART'S MUSIC SHOP: COLUMBUS, GA
BAHAMA PAWN: PANAMA CITY BEACH, FL
BAILEY BROTHERS MUSIC: MONTGOMERY, AL
BAMA PAWN SHOP: MONTGOMERY, AL
BAY PAWN & GOLD: PENSACOLA, FL
BEST PAWN & EXCHANGE: MONTGOMERY, AL
BIG JOHN'S PAWN SHOP: SELMA, AL
BOATNER'S: STANDING ROCK, AL
DALLAS BRYANT: BRUNDIDGE, AL
JIM BUCH, JR.: MONTGOMERY, AL
BURDETT'S PAWN SHOP: ANNISTON, AL
CAHABA JEWELRY & LOAN: BIRMINGHAM, AL
TIM & DONALD CANNON: WEOKA, AL
CAPITOL PAWN SHOP: MONTGOMERY, AL
CAPITOL MUSIC CENTER: MONTGOMERY, AL
CARSON'S PAWN SHOP: PENSACOLA, FL
CHISOLM GUN & PAWN; MONTGOMERY, AL
CAROL & BOB CHRISTOPHER; DECATUR, AL
CITY PAWN SHOP: ALEXANDER CITY, AL
CMC: COLUMBUS, GA
COLAIANNI MUSIC CO.: COLUMBUS, GA
COLUMBUS PAWN SHOP: COLUMBUS, GA
THE COMMON SHOP: FLORALA, AL
CRESTVIEW PAWN SHOP: CRESTVIEW, FL
D & D GOLD & SILVER TRADERS: OZARK, AL
D & S ELECTRONICS: FORT WALTON BEACH, FL
DIXIE GUITARS: SMYRNA, GA
PEE WEE DUTTON; MONTGOMERY, AL
DYESS MUSIC CENTER: OPP, AL
EAST ALBANY PAWN SHOP: ALBANY, GA
EUFAULA JEWELERS: EUFAULA, AL
EZ PAWN & LOAN: SYLACAUGA, AL
FLASH GUITARS: ANNISTON, AL
FORT DALE PAWN SHOP: GREENVILLE, AL
FRIDAY'S PAWN SHOP: CRESTVIEW, FL
FRITZ BROTHERS GUITARS: MOBILE, AL
GALLOWAY GOLD: ANNISTON, AL
GARDEN STREET PAWN SHOP: PENSACOLA, FL
GENEVA DISCOUNT & PAWN: GENEVA, AL
GEORGIA INSURANCE & LOAN: ALBANY, GA
GEORGIA LOAN CO: ALBANY, GA
GEORGIA LOAN & PAWN SHOP: ALBANY, GA
GEORGIA PAWN SHOP: LAGRANGE, GA
GOLD MINE PAWN: DAPHNE, AL
GOLDEN EAGLE PAWN SHOP: DALEVILLE, AL
GORDY'S MUSIC: FERNDALE, MI
GORDY'S SWAP SHOP: LAGRANGE, GA
GUITAR GALLERY: TUSCALOOSA, AL
GUITAR SHOPPE: AUBURN, AL
HALEY LIGHTNING SOUND: PENSACOLA, FL
HALL'S PAWN SHOP: SOMERSET, KY
JAMIE HAMILTON: PRATTVILLE, AL
HARRIS MUSIC: PENSACOLA, FL

HERB'S JEWELERS: COLUMBUS, GA
HUB CITY PAWN SHOP: CRESTVIEW, FL
JACK'S JEWELERS, INC.: COLUMBUS, GA
JIMMY'S MENS STORE & PAWN SHOP: FORT WALTON BEACH, FL
CHARLES JOHNSON: PANAMA CITY, FL
JOE JONES PAWN: ENTERPRISE, AL
KEN'S PAWN SHOP: CRESTVIEW, FL
KWIK KASH PAWN SHOP: PANAMA CITY, FL
L.A. GUN & PAWN: BONIFAY, FL
L.A. INSTRUMENT REPAIR: DOTHAN, AL
LUKE & SONS: ANNISTON, AL
LYNAM'S TRADING POST: MONROEVILLE, AL
LYNN'S CASH & CARRY; EUFAULA, AL
M & M PAWN SHOP: PENSACOLA, FL
MACKEY'S COLLECTIBLES: GREENVILLE, AL
STEVE MANESS: WETUMPKA, AL
MAX'S DISCOUNT JEWELERS: MONTGOMERY, AL
PAUL MAYER: MOBILE, AL
McPEAKE'S UNIQUE INSTRUMENTS: MT. JULIET, TN
METRO MUSIC: DOTHAN, AL
METRO PAWNBROKERS: ALBANY, GA
METRO PAWNBROKERS: SMYRNA, GA
MIDTOWN MUSIC: ATLANTA, GA
MIKE'S MUSIC: FORT WALTON BEACH, FL
MILLHOUSE PAWN SHOP: GROVE HILL, AL
MILTON GOLD & SILVER EXCHANGE: MILTON, FL
DONNIE MIMS: MONTGOMERY, AL
MIRACLE STRIP PAWN SHOP: PANAMA CITY BEACH, FL
MUSIC CONNECTION: PRATTVILLE, AL
MUSIC DEPOT: LAGRANGE, GA
MUSIC MATTERS: MONTGOMERY, AL
MUSIC TRADER: PANAMA CITY, FL
ANDY NOEL: MONTGOMERY, AL
NORTHWEST SERVICE ENTERPRISES: SMYRNA, GA
ROBERT ORR: AUBURN, AL
RELFE PARKER JR.: WETUMPKA, AL
PACE BLVD. PAWN: PENSACOLA, FL
PARK N' PAWN: PENSACOLA, FL
LUTHER PETERS: OZARK, AL
PHENIX PAWN SHOP: PHENIX CITY, AL
QUALITY JEWELERS & LOAN, INC.: PANAMA CITY, FL
RAVEN MUSIC: DOTHAN, AL
MAX REEVES: TROY, AL
BILLY RICE: ASHFORD, AL
RICK'S GUN & PAWN & GUN: FOLEY, AL
ROCK & HOCK PAWN & MUSIC: PANAMA CITY, FL
S & W PAWN AND JEWELRY CO.: PANAMA CITY BEACH, FL
GRADY SANDERS: WETUMPKA, AL
SILVER MINE: FORT WALTON BEACH, FL
SILVER MINE: PENSACOLA, FL
SOMERSET PAWN SHOP: SOMERSET, KY
BARRY STAPP: SELMA, AL
STRINGS & THINGS: ANDALUSIA, AL
TOMMY SULLIVAN: MONTGOMERY, AL
TOP DOLLAR PAWN: FORT WALTON BEACH, FL
TRADING POST PAWN SHOP: FORT WALTON BEACH, FL
TRADING POST PAWN: PANAMA CITY, FL
UPTOWN PAWN SHOP: COLUMBUS, GA
VALLEY PAWN SHOP: VALLEY, AL
GRADY WAKEFIELD: NEWELL, AL
BOBBY WALKER: OZARK, AL
WEST MAIN JEWELRY & LOAN: DOTHAN, AL
MIKE WHISENANT: LACEY'S SPRINGS, AL
WIREGRASS MUSIC: ENTERPRISE, AL

NOTE: Some persons (who wish to remain anonymous) submitted photographs that were used in the photo section; however, approximately 98% of these photographs were taken by the author.

Contents

Foreword

By   Stan Jay,
President of Mandolin Brothers, Ltd

The love of guitars (or, more precisely, American fretted instruments) makes Romantics of us all. From George Harrison ("While My Guitar Gently Weeps") to James Taylor ("Me and My Guitar, always in the same mood, I am mostly flesh and blood while he is mostly wood...")* we ascribe feelings to the (supposedly) inanimate device and, at the same time, we are elevated and made joyous by its inescapable power to inspire us and make us expressive. Hopefully, every person who reads this book is interested in starting and/or maintaining a close, long relationship with a guitar (or guitars) and feels, as I do every time I hold one, that little burst of inner happiness (not unlike chewing gum with a flavor capsule in the middle) that you get when the guitar is in its playing position and your fingers are poised to strike the strings. Guitars - - from Danelectros to Martin abalone trimmed prewar D-45's - - enchant us when we play, heft, hold, smell, caress, scrutinize and gaze at them, and when we marvel at the unpretentious perfection of their design. We feel extra good when, appreciative of this complexity of information, we get to retain, and become a caretaker for (some people say "own"), an especially fine example.

Owning our guitars, playing them, or obsessing on them, the way many of us do, somehow defines each of us beyond that which we do for a living, how many kids we have or don't have, or whether we own a house and one or more cars. Guitars, and the music played upon them, give structure to our lives. When used for performance, whether we play an acoustic 1941 Gibson L5-P (Premiere - the original cutaway series) archtop jazz guitar, softly, without a pick, or launch the sonic shrapnel of a screaming 1960 Stratocaster, wide open with the volume knob of the matching white cabinet Bandmaster amplifier brazed to "10", we control, to a great extent, the environment we ourselves create in that room, auditorium or stadium. By comparison, simply possessing one of these collectible guitars (in very good condition or better, of course) makes us feel (a) that we are the envy of all the friends, relatives, vintage dealers, other guitar owners whom we don't actually know and the rest of the population of the earth, (b) that, both while we're playing it and during those periods when we're not, we have continuous access to one of the finest examples of a musical instrument of its kind in existence, (c) that we deserve to have such access due to our having, to date, led an exemplary, wholesome, morally correct life and (d) that we have made a wise investment decision which will result, ultimately, in our (or our heirs) exchanging this dried and venerable hard fibrous xylem for higher denominations of the mint green paper we call money then we (or our skeptical spouses) ever thought possible.

What, then, does that make the guitar collector: the person who accumulates, for his or her personal pleasure (Can the perception of pleasure be anything but personal?), the fretted instruments produced within the past 16 decades of American manufacturing? And, one may wonder, what rights and responsibilities are his who embraces this role? What compilation of arcane knowledge and important caveats should one carry with him while on the quest? (You should never, well, almost never, leave on a quest without atleast one caveat in your wallet and several more in the pocket of your guitar case.) Ah yes, the answers to these and many questions lie beyond... that is, beyond this Foreword, in the book you are holding.

That you have acquired this primer is a good beginning. As a human trained to be a teacher of college English (turned mandolin mogul and global guitar guide) I can tell you three important things: read, read and read. The bibliography (it's at the end - - turn to it now to consider its majestic serenity) lists 20-some titles, the perusal of which you may consider your homework assignment. Subscribing to the various magazines cited within these pages is also an excellent idea - - the subscriptions are inexpensive, the knowledge gained, priceless. There's an old saying, gleaned from the antiques business, which I've taken to heart and bring up when counseling folks who already own, wish to find, or wish to sell, fine vintage fretted American instruments (which is my job, and I love it - I tell people that I haven't gone to work in 20 years) and that saying is "The More You Know, The Luckier You Get." If you can remember even one-quarter of the information contained within this book and the others suggested, you are more than likely to "discover" wonderful guitars, get better deals, reject the instruments which have serious deficiencies, understand why some examples are special and other mundane and, hopefully, learn to take the best care of that which you acquire (especially by not altering it in <u>any</u> way if it is original to start with). One more thing: as Polonius told his son, Laertes, "Costly thy habit as thy purse can buy, but not expressed in fancy; rich, not gaudy." of course, he was talking about buying clothes at the Mall. I prefer to interpret this advice as "Save up your money so that you can afford higher-end, better quality, more desirable, durable, investment-level instruments instead of blowing it on cheap, flashy, (frequently imported) stuff." If you accept this assignment and these responsibilities, and do the, required reading, then you can (and should) go off into the world of Master Models, Martins and Mosrites, wallets at the ready and <u>buy</u>!

Stan with two great American guitars,
Top: 1934 Martin D-28, Bottom: 1941 Martin D-45

"Thassa Gibson. Thassa collector's item", said the pawn shop owner.

"Uh-huh. And I'm Chet Atkins", I thought to myself. True, he was referring to a 1976 Gibson Bicentennial Firebird, which was supposed to be a limited edition that was Gibson's contribution to America's 200th birthday; the Bicentennial Firebird ultimately turned out to be the biggest production run of that body style in Gibson's history up to that point.

The reason my mental response was so sarcastic was that the pawn shop owner thought that simply because the guitar was a Gibson product, it was worth a good deal more than most of the other instruments in his store. He **didn't** know that it was a Bicentennial edition, and also what he apparently didn't know (or wouldn't acknowledge) was that the guitar was in such terrible condition (worn finish, warped scratchplate, corroded hardware) that it was worthless to anyone with a legitimate interest in vintage American fretted instruments.

The purpose of this book is not to "burst someone's bubble" about an instrument or instruments that he/she might believe is a valuable piece when in fact it isn't. I'm a strong believer in ethics, which admittedly is all too often missing in many facets of the music business, and as one who "cut his musical teeth" during the "Guitar Boom" of the Sixties, I've seen increasing interest in even some of the promotional or "house brand" guitars from that era. Accordingly, I feel that it's important to keep information on American-made guitars and basses as accurate and honest as possible, **particularly** since American-made fretted instruments now account for only about **ten percent** of all guitars and basses sold in the U.S. each year. Times have sure changed.

Please understand that yours truly considers himself to be an **average** player and an **average** collector ("so maybe that makes you an average **writer** as well", says Malc, who's my musical and philosophical peer). At any rate, I don't make my living from playing music, nor do I read music (looks like birds on a wire to me), and my somewhat modest collection of American-made instruments consists of token examples of several classic guitars and basses; i.e., I have one Fender Stratocaster, one Rickenbacker 4001 bass, etc. As of this writing I've just about "maxxed out" with the types that I've garnered, and may in the future opt to recycle certain models if I encounter a cleaner or rarer example. I will, however, admit to a penchant for natural-finished, translucent-finished, or sunburst-finished instruments. Any guitar or bass that has the grain showing instantly gets more interest from this part-time player/collector.

There are many fine books available concerning the history of American instruments, as well as instructional books offering playing guidance (not to mention instructional audio cassettes and videotapes). However, it occurred to me that I play and collect primarily for the **enjoyment and interest**, and I feel that there's a need for a handbook for people who are in the same situation as me. Some folks' "interest" in guitars and basses may have a financial motive (pawn shops, for example), while others may want to find out about whether something they own (or used to own) might be of historical and/or financial value.

I'll be the first to admit that this book won't have all the answers to questions some readers may have. That's why I would encourage anyone who is curious about a particular instrument that he or she owns (or has encountered) to contact a vintage retailer or guitar buff for accurate information (in the case of finer pieces, a signed and dated **appraisal** is highly recommended). There is also a growing number of highly-detailed guitar books that can be consulted. While much of the information contained herein is the result of catalog research as well as phone calls and letters to vintage authorities and instrument manufacturers, I also own a copy of every book listed in this handbook's bibliography.

Of course, I've also subscribed to periodicals such as Guitar Player, Guitar World and Bass Player; many times these magazines will have informative articles about older or unique instruments. Moreover, much of the research I've done myself has ended up in Vintage Guitar magazine, for which I write feature articles and an monthly column (from the perspective of an "aging rock 'n roller").

Some readers might be disappointed that only American-made guitars and basses will be addressed; that's because they generally tend to be the most desirable. Please excuse my jingoism, but I've determined that the plethora of foreign-made fretted instruments is too complex to be researched. Most are usually cheap copies of American instruments anyway, and the only time I will discuss imported guitars and basses will be when name licensing is noted with a particular brand, or whenever a counterfeit or forgery is described.

Moreover, for the sake of brevity and simplicity, fretted instruments and stringed instruments other than Spanish-style guitars and basses will not be addressed in this handbook; such instruments include banjos, lap steels, mandolins, violins, fiddles, steel guitars, etc. Such instruments are more specialized when it comes to both information **and** demand, and there are many resources (books, vintage authorities, etc.) that can be consulted.

Solidbody instruments will receive more attention herein than will flat-top or archtop guitars and basses. There are more solidbody styles and brands around, but admittedly, growing up in the Sixties guitar boom (which generally involved solidbody instruments) may have influenced this decision. Archtop guitars are stereotypically associated with jazz players, and flat-tops are stereotypically associated with Country - and - Western players. Solidbodies, on the other hand, are usually found in the hands of a rock 'n roller more than any other instrument. Let me emphasize that acoustics will not be neglected but will be addressed more generally, and there are several fine books available concerning specific brands of acoustic instruments. For what it's worth, my aforementioned "modest" collection does not include a full-depth jazz-type electric acoustic such as a Gibson ES-175, and I'd love to have one. Acoustic guitars, as well as their electric variations, represent probably the highest echelon of guitar craftsmanship, and that can't help but be respected by any guitar enthusiast, even one with rock 'n roll roots.

I'm also going to decline to discuss **price** in this handbook; admittedly I don't want to overlap with any of the price-oriented books that are already out there, but I also feel that price is all too often overemphasized. I interviewed the noted vintage authority George Gruhn of Nashville in the Spring of 1990, and he stated that the price of some instruments can change by as much as **100% in six months**, which means that any market that volatile probably shouldn't have pricing information published that shows any kind of rigid structuring, because such pricing could be outdated very quickly. Gruhn also feels (as do I) that it would be nice for some U.S. vintage enthusiasts to seek out American instruments because of their historical value instead of the "how much can I get for it" mentality that is all to often found among certain vintage guitar retailers. It might surprise many people to learn that many of the finer vintage American guitars and basses end up being exported to Japan and Europe!

One other thing that I hope the reader will understand is that when **opinions** are encountered in this book, said opinions will have facts to back them up, just as the **information** contained in this book is as accurate as the facts I've been able to compile.

Literary purists may get agitated that yours truly will tend to write in the first person at various times in this handbook. With all due respect to such folks, so what? I consider myself to be a vintage guitar enthusiast, so perhaps my "enthusiasm" makes me want to write about guitars like I'm having a conversation with the reader, citing my own experiences with classic pieces of fretted American instruments.

In my dealings with pawn shops, flea markets and individuals in my area of the country, I've discovered that many people are not familiar with the basic parts found on fretted instruments, so that seemed like a logical place to start:

Parts of the Guitar

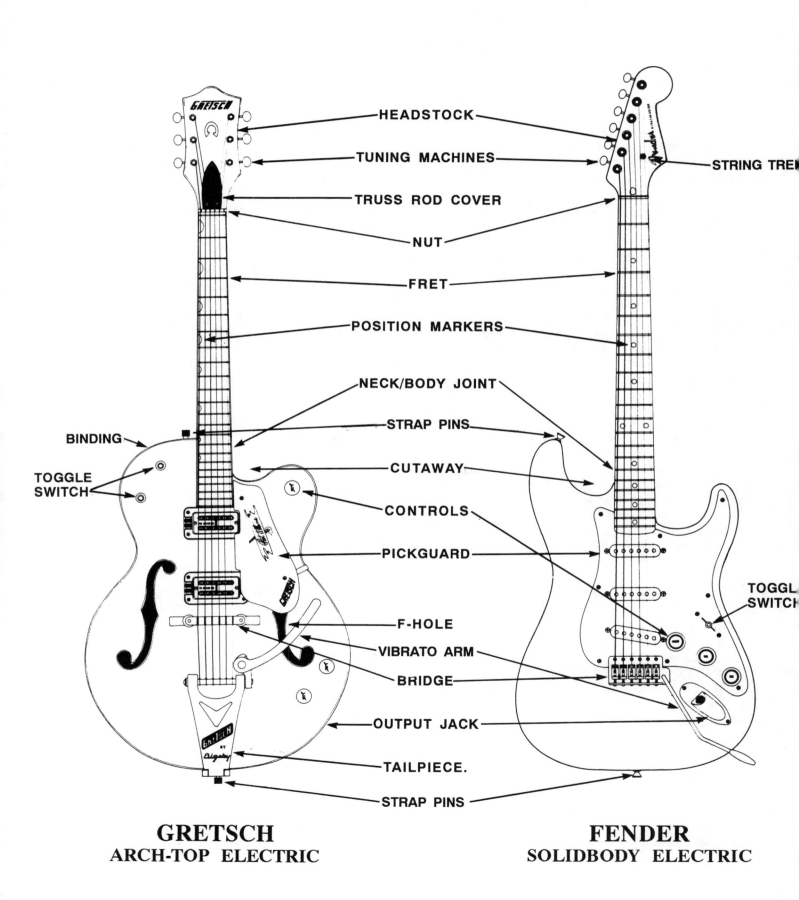

HEADSTOCK

TUNING MACHINES

STRING TRE

TRUSS ROD COVER

NUT

FRET

POSITION MARKERS

NECK/BODY JOINT

BINDING

STRAP PINS

TOGGLE SWITCH

CUTAWAY

CONTROLS

PICKGUARD

TOGGLE SWITCH

F-HOLE

VIBRATO ARM

BRIDGE

OUTPUT JACK

TAILPIECE.

STRAP PINS

GRETSCH
ARCH-TOP ELECTRIC

FENDER
SOLIDBODY ELECTRIC

Guitar drawings courtesy 20th Century Guitar

GUITAR-OLOGY 101

1. GUITAR STYLES and PARTS

For the purpose of keeping things simple, any reference to "guitar" will actually be a reference to "guitar or bass" unless otherwise noted.

Acoustic (non-electric) guitars come in two body styles:
- A. **Flat-top**: Standard type of guitar with a round soundhole.
- B. **Arch-top**: Curved top with two "f-holes" (as found on violins, cellos, etc.) instead of a round soundhole. This body style may be spelled as "archtop" or "arch-top".

Electric guitars come in several body styles:
- A. **Flat-top electric**: Simply a flat-top acoustic with an added "pickup" (to be defined in the next section). Not too many flat-tops have factory-installed electronics, and those that do usually have the pickup concealed (Ovation guitars usually have this feature). Many pickups can be purchased as accessories and installed by players.
- B. **Arch-top electric**: As is the case with flat-top electronics, basically an acoustic instrument with added electronics. However, while there are more acoustic flat-tops than there are acoustic arch-tops, the reverse is true with acoustic-electric guitars; many arch-tops come from the factory fully laden with electronic features. A classic example of an arch-top electric is the Gibson ES-175.
- C. **Solid-body electric**: Exactly what it says it is, and by far the most popular type of electric guitar. Almost always, the body is made of wood; however, the Eighties saw the advent of guitars made from space-age composite materials by Ned Steinberger (actually, Steinberger bass guitars preceded their six-string guitars). Some promotional guitars from the Sixties, such as Gibson's Kalamazoo line, had bodies that were made of molded chipboard! As is the case with "archtop"/"arch-top", the body style's name may be spelled with or without a hyphen ("solidbody" or "solid-body").
- D. **Semi-solid electric**: An attempt to combine the best features of arch-top electrics and solid-body electronics. The pioneering Gibson ES-335 (introduced in 1958) is a definitive example. Semi-solids have a thinner depth than arch-top electrics, and contain a solid piece of wood inside, which is supposed to feature better ambience like a solid-body instrument, yet the semi-solid is of lighter weight. Please note that some arch-top electrics may come in thinner versions as well as full-depth styles. The semi-solid guitar should feel a bit heavier, of course, but I'd still recommend that the inside of the instrument be examined (through one of the f-holes) to see if there is a block of wood, which would designate it as a semi-solid rather than a thin-line version of an arch-top electric. Many people refer to "semi-solid electric guitars" as "semi-hollow guitars".

So much for styles of guitars; now let's take a look at the parts that make up an individual instrument.

TUNING MACHINES: Tuning keys (six on guitars, four on basses)

HEADSTOCK: End of instrument where tuning keys are located. (Except Steinberger, and Licensed-by-Steinberger, whose tuners, for the most part, are on the body end.)

STRING TREE: Extra reinforcement for thinner strings; such strings pass under string tree. Many guitars do not have string trees, so don't think an instrument is missing one if you can't find it.

TRUSS ROD COVER: Most guitars have a solid metal truss rod inside the neck that runs the full length of the neck to prevent warpage. Truss rods are usually adjustable with a socket wrench or screwdriver, but **such adjustments should only be done by a qualified guitar technician!** If a truss rod is over-torqued, the rod or neck can break, ruining the instrument. In some cases, the truss rod adjustment is located at the joint of the neck and body, and the neck must usually be detached to perform the adjustment. Most of the time, however, a bell-shaped piece of plastic on the headstock covers the location where the truss rod can be adjusted.

NUT: Made of grooved plastic, bone, graphite, or metal; all strings pass through the nut then diverge to individual tuning machines.

11

FRET: The distance between each of these wire strips changes the pitch of each string by one note (same as black keys and white keys on a keyboard instrument).

POSITION MARKER: Indicates specific notes on specific strings.

CUTAWAY: Contoured portion of the body that creates a "horn" on the side; designed for easier access to upper register of each string. Guitar bodies may be non-cutaway (as is the case with most acoustic instruments), single-cutaway (as shown on the Gretsch arch-top electric), or double-cutaway (as shown on the Fender solid-body electric).

NECK/BODY JOINT: Neck is either glued or bolted on here. In some cases, neck runs all the way through to the end of the instrument, and body sides are simply glued onto it.

BINDING: White, beige or black material that "binds" wood edges together.

PICKGUARD: Hard, thin material (usually plastic) designed to prevent the guitar pick from damaging the finish. Also known as a "scratchplate". Pickguards are mounted in either an "elevated" position (as found on most arch-top guitars) or "flush" (as found on most solid-body and flat-top guitars).

F-HOLE: As previously noted, a soundhole found on arch-top guitars.

CONTROLS: Volume and tone potentiometers. Sometimes such controls are arranged so that there is one volume "pot" and one tone "pot" for each pickup (offering the greatest variety of sounds); other instruments feature a master volume control and a master tone control.

TOGGLE SWITCH: Turns specific pickups off and on. Obviously this device would not be found on a single-pickup instrument. In many cases, sliding switches that operate individual pickups will be found on guitars instead of a toggle switch.

OUTPUT JACK: Cord to amplifier plugs in here.

BRIDGE: Grooved passage for strings; in many cases there is an individual "saddle" for each string, allowing for more precise tuning.

VIBRATO ARM: A spring-loaded mechanism designed to vary pitch. May be original equipment or add-on accessory.

TAILPIECE: "Ball" end of string anchors here. On many guitars, bridge and tailpiece are combined into a single unit.

STRAP PIN(S): Guitar strap attaches here.

> **NOTE:** There are some parts found on other types of instruments that are not shown on these guitars; among such important parts are:

BELLY CUT/WAIST CONTOUR: Grooved area cut into the backside of a solid-body guitar for comfort. Not all solid-body guitars have this feature.

THUMB REST: Short wooden or plastic strip found on the "bass" side of a bass guitar body (which is the side with the thicker strings). Exactly what it says it is.

FINGER REST: Found on the "treble" side of a bass guitar body (where the thinner strings are located). Exactly what it says it is; usually bass guitars will have either a thumb rest or a finger rest, but some oddball basses will have both.

2. SCALES

The "scale" of a guitar or bass **is the distance from the nut to the bridge**. As a general rule, most guitar scales range from 24" to 25 1/2"; anything shorter is usually considered a 3/4 scale instrument and would normally be found on promotional/beginners' guitars.

However, the scales found on bass guitars are more varied, and as such can present a more complex situation. The normal guidelines for bass scales can be divided into three lengths:

SHORT SCALE:	30" - 30 1/2"
MEDIUM SCALE:	32"
FULL/LONG SCALE:	34" (some rare basses have even longer scales!)

Again, **even shorter scales** can be found on 3/4 size basses, but it helps to know **almost all bass guitars come in full 34" scale**. Short-scale bass guitars are far less popular than they were in the past, and **bass strings designed for a full-scale instrument should not be used on basses with a short or medium scale**, due to the possibility of breakage. The selection of strings designed to fit short-scale and medium-scale basses is somewhat limited (some types will fit either medium-scale or full-scale), and it is not completely out of line to opine that such smaller basses are going the route of 8-track tape players or Beta video recorders (perhaps a more contemporary comparison would be record turntables, as vinyl LPs gradually lurch toward extinction, being replaced by cassettes and compact discs).

Examples of once-popular short-scale basses that are now out of production include Gibson's "EB" series, and Fender Musicmaster and Mustang basses. Medium-scale basses are even rarer, and are usually found on higher-end instruments such as those made by Alembic and Phillip Kubicki. The Robin "Ranger" is a relatively rare example of a more reasonably-priced 32" scale bass. Accordingly, pawn shops might want to consider measuring the scale of a bass guitar that is brought in for a loan; use your experience with the aforementioned 8-track tape players and Beta VCRs as a guideline, as short-scale and medium-scale basses also appear to be a vanishing breed.

3. PICKUPS

As previously noted earlier in this chapter, the essential component of an electric guitar or bass is the pickup, which senses the vibrations of strings. Not only can pickups be found in **assorted quantities** on particular instruments, but they also come in several **different designs**, the most popular of which will be examined more closely herein.

A pickup mainly consists of a magnet and wiring inside a specialized housing (see the Danelectro section of the chapter on American brand names for details on a bizarre pickup used by that particular company). The main two types found on instruments today are "single coil" and "double coil (humbucking)". Single coil pickups have one unit involving the previously noted parts. They are usually oval-shaped and brighter-sounding than "humbuckers". Examples include pickups found on most Fender electrics, and Gibson's P-90, which has six "polepieces" (screws) centered in the pickup's middle (P-90s usually have covers that are black plastic, although cream-colored and metal-covered P-90s have also been made).

Gibson patented the "humbucking" pickup in the 1950s; the concept of having two coils in a pickup at reverse polarity to each other meant that unwanted electrical interference would be eliminated (hence the name for the pickup). As a general rule, most humbucking pickups measure approximately 2 3/4 " x 1 1/2", and if they have polepieces/screws projecting through their covers, such polepieces/screws are usually located along one of the longer sides of the cover's surface.

Some exceptions to these general guidelines can include humbucking pickups with **twelve** exposed polepieces/screws (as found on some Gretsch instruments) or of course **no** exposed polepieces/screws. Some humbuckers may be smaller (not surprisingly, they are known as "mini-humbuckers"), and may have polepieces (as found on the Gibson Les Paul Deluxe) or may not (as found on certain Gibson Firebirds and SGs). As might be expected, humbucking pickups have the reputation of sounding "mellower" or "bluesier" than single coil models, and mini-humbuckers are supposedly a bit brighter-sounding than regular size humbuckers.

Another area where pickups and an instrument's tonal properties are intertwined concerns a pickup's location on an instrument. If a pickup is located near the neck/body joint, it will give the instrument a mellow, jazz-like tone. On the other hand, a pickup located towards the bridge offers the player a more trebly, biting sound. Thus, the more pickups that are on an instrument, the greater variety of sounds the instrument will be able to provide. Mention needs to be made here of the "concept" of removing pickup covers in order to evoke a better sound from an instrument. Studies have shown that the sound of a guitar or bass does not change if pickup covers are removed. This "idea" is usually done on instruments with regular size humbucking pickups, and in some cases companies such as Gibson have marketed guitars without pickup covers over humbucking units, in which case such pickups are called "open-coil humbuckers". It is recommended that if a player chooses to remove pickup covers, the covers should be retained so as not to devalue the instrument.

4. GUITARS VS. BASS GUITARS: THE DIFFERENCES

Some time ago, one pawn shop wanted to know how to tell the difference between "regular guitars" (his phrase) and bass guitars. I pointed out that cosmetically the things to look for include such things as a bass guitar being longer and having only four strings. Nowadays, however, there are such items as five-string and even six-string bass guitars, as bass guitar technology grew by leaps and bounds in the Eighties.

Bass guitars are supposed to serve not only as musical instruments that play notes, they also serve to help keep the beat of a song; in a combo setting the bass and drums are referred to as the "rhythm section". Bass guitar strings are of course much thicker than guitar strings, and they are picked or plucked one note at a time. Guitars, on the other hand, may be strummed as a "rhythm" guitar, and/or they can function as a "lead" guitar, playing the actual melody of a tune.

In times past, there have been some attempts by some manufacturers to market "baritone guitars", which had six strings but were tuned an octave lower. Such instruments included Fender's Bass VI and Gibson's EB-6. While interesting, they were not successful and are not particularly desirable in the vintage market as utility instruments, but they do merit some interest by some collectors as historical pieces.

Five-string and six-string basses that are marketed today are usually higher-end items, oriented toward professional players; i.e., don't expect too many of these to show up in pawn shops. If a six-string bass does happen to come in, it should be measured as previously noted. Baritone guitars had **short** scales; current models of six-string basses are almost exclusively **full-scale**. The vast majority of guitars that are seen in pawn shops are, of course, "regular guitars", and the basses encountered are almost always four-string models, but it helps knowing about some of the features inherent with each style, as it could affect loan value and/or retail value.

5. ACTIVE ELECTRONICS

One last (and relatively new) feature of both guitars and basses that needs to be addressed is "active electronics". The folks at Alembic claim to have been the first to incorporate the concept of active electronics into fretted instruments (in 1969). Until that time, all electric guitars and basses had been "passive", although the term itself probably didn't exist. Simply put, passive electric guitars and basses are ones that have simple volume and tone controls; usually the control knobs are calibrated "1" through "10".

On the other hand, instruments with active electronics have some kind of solid-state circuitry built into them; such circuitry is designed to enhance the instrument's sound and is usually powered by a replaceable 9-volt battery that installs in the back. Active circuitry can give a guitar or bass more "gain" (loose translation: "punch") and/or can expand the tone spectrum of an instrument in several different ways; either the tone pots are given more range, and/or some added switches can boost and cut certain frequencies. Among the innovations found on some active instruments are tone knobs calibrated from "0" to "5" **in both clockwise and counter-clockwise directions** (indicating a boost or cut in the tone), and a small LED that lights up on the face of the instrument whenever the cord is plugged in, indicating that the active circuitry is working (and the battery is being used).

Types of active circuitry can vary with individual manufacturers and models, and, as might be expected, such instruments tend to be oriented towards active (no pun intended) professional musicians; an average player would probably tend to be confused by the extra "gizmos" available. While it's too soon to tell if certain instruments with certain types of active electronics will ultimately become desirable, so far the trend in the used guitar market seems to indicate that active electronics is not that much of an extra feature, unless of course as previously stated the instrument is used in a professional environment.

In summary, this is of course a very simplistic overview of the construction and function of Spanish-type guitars and basses, and hopefully it has been somewhat enlightening. Many other facets could be examined (for example, "classical" flat-top acoustics use nylon or gut strings instead of steel strings, and classical guitars usually do not have fret markers), but rather than try to make the reader feel like he/she needs to become a Ph.D in Guitar Information, this basic course should serve as a foundation from which to judge instruments that the reader may encounter.

Class dismissed.

AMERICAN GUITAR BRAND NAMES:
A GENERAL GUIDE

This alphabetized list contains American guitar brand names that may have been painstakingly handmade (D'Angelico, Stromberg) or cranked out by the truckload (Harmony, Kay). Only American brand names will be cited, and in the case of where a brand name was made in the U.S. but is now either being made exclusively overseas under name licensing, or in some cases is being made domestically **and** overseas, the reader will be alerted as to such.

Admittedly there may be some omissions to this list; such names left out may be obscure house brands or small companies that specialize in handmade and/or custom-order guitars. Moreover, the reader should also note that many of the brands on this list **may never show up in a pawn shop.** Some of these brands existed in the 1800s only!

However, no foreign instrument without "U.S. roots" will be noted, so don't expect to see the names of lines like Hofner (Germany), Hagstrom (Sweden), Vox or Eko (Italy) listed; nor will any of the myriad of Far East imports be noted (Ibanez, Aria, Tokai, Global, Hondo, Bentley, Cort, etc.). While many of these companies manufacture a very fine product, they generally aren't very popular among guitar enthusiasts, except as utility instruments in some cases.

Gibson and Fender are so diverse and popular that they will be addressed in separate chapters.

A: This single letter is found on some budget instruments and is attributed to Aldens, a department store chain that is now out of business

ACOUSTIC: This company marketed a guitar and bass known as the "Black Widow" from 1972-1973. Some were made by Semie Moseley (see Mosrite), others in Japan. Bartell also reportedly made some Acoustic brand instruments. Acoustic was known primarily for their amplifier line, and this fretted instrument foray was unsuccessful.

AIRLINE: House brand name for Montgomery Ward guitars that were usually made by Harmony, Kay or Valco. Some foreign-made instruments may also have been marketed in the late Sixties.

ALAMO: Inexpensive, promotional line dating from the Fifties. May have been a house brand at one time.

ALEMBIC: Very high-priced instruments (primarily basses) made in San Francisco area, using all sorts of exotic hardwoods (vermillion, zebrawood, Hawaiian flame koa, etc.). Many of the Alembics made are custom-ordered, one-of-a-kind instruments. Sometimes the company name may not appear on an instrument's headstock, but its **logo** does, which is **a hand reaching out of a cloud, gripping a teardrop-shaped object.** This headstock logo is in stainless steel. An Alembic's serial number should be found on the fretboard near the neck/body joint; usually the first two numbers indicate the year of production.

ALMCRANTZ: Flat-top line from the turn of the century.

ALOHA: House brand for a Chicago-based publishing and musical instrument company; instruments were most likely made by Chicago-area manufacturers.

AMPEG: Also an attempt by an amplifier company to get into the guitar biz; their first instrument was marketed in 1962. Their solidbody scroll-head basses are notable (one has **f-holes that go all the way through the body!**), but their most popular series was the Dan Armstrong-designed line of lucite-bodied guitars and basses, commonly known as the See Throughs, since they were clear in color. Ampeg also marketed some English guitars and basses (made by Burns) during the Sixties.

ARMSTRONG, DAN: See AMPEG.

ANDERSEN STRINGED INSTRUMENTS: Very high-priced instruments, hand made in Seattle, WA by Steven Andersen

ATLAS: House brand seen on Valco-made instrument.

AUDITION: F.W. Woolworth/Woolco house brand. All of the instruments that have been encountered by the author have been imports.

B & G: A New Jersey distributor that sold Danelectro-made instruments; one of the rare examples where another name is found on a Danelectro guitar or bass other than Silvertone, Coral or Danelectro itself.

15

B & J: New York distributor that put its name on several promotional instruments.

BACON & DAY (B&D): Originally a banjo company that was sold to Gretsch in the Thirties; supposedly there was also some type of manufacturing arrangement with Regal, so it appears that Bacon & Day guitars may have been made by both Gretsch and Regal.

BALDWIN: The famous piano manufacturer marketed a line of guitars, basses and amplifiers in the Sixties, but **all guitars and basses were made by Burns (of London, England)**; i.e., there is no such thing as a domestically-made Baldwin guitar, unless certain prototypes exist.

BALL, ERNIE: Known primarily as a source for strings and picks. Some Ernie Ball "Earthwood" acoustic guitars and acoustic bass guitars were marketed in the Seventies. Acoustic bass guitars were rare in the fretted instrument field at the time, although many companies market such instruments as of this writing. Accordingly, Earthwood basses are interesting as a curiosity item. Currently, Ernie Ball manufactures Music Man instruments.

BARTELL: Rare California solidbodies by Paul Barth, who was also associated at times with National, Rickenbacker and Magnatone. Bartell also made other brands (including some Acoustics?).

BAUER: Associated with S.S. Stewart of Philadelphia in the late 1800s; made durable flat-tops. The name later appeared in the 1930s and 1940s on promotional instruments, probably due to name licensing.

BAY STATE: An 1800s line associated with Haumes, Ditson and Tilton. Intricate and nicely-made instruments.

BEAN, TRAVIS: Innovative, California-made instruments featuring aluminum necks. Made from 1974-1979.

BELTONE: Very inexpensive promotional line; marketers of a guitar with a fake resonator plate (like a Dobro)! Some Premier-made instruments may have been marketed. The name may also be spelled BELL-TONE.

BENEDETTO: Modern, exquisite hand-made archtop brand.

BIGSBY: Although known almost exclusively for his innovations on vibrato arms installed on guitars, Paul Bigsby made some primitive solidbody instruments in the late Forties; in fact, there has been an ongoing controversy for years as to whether or not Leo Fender "borrowed" some of Bigsby's ideas. Much of the input into Bigsby's designs are credited to famed player Merle Travis.

BOEHM: Early Twentieth-Century brand about which little is known; some instruments may have been made by Washburn.

BOGUE, REX: California guitar maker who created custom instruments for the like of Mahavishnu John McLaughlin. Very ornate workmanship; likewise very expensive. The style of Rex Bogue's instruments was copied by Ibanez on an imported series.

BORYS: Exquisite hollow-body line hand-made in Burlington, Vermont, specializing in a "Jazz Electric" version (hollow-body or semi-solid styles) and a "Jazz Acoustic" arch top. Only about 20 guitars are made per year.

BOZO: Made near San Diego, primarily expensive flat-tops with ornate features.

BRADFORD: House brand for W.T. Grant department stores. Most of what is seen of these are imports.

BRUNO: Originally associated with Martin in the 1800s, now a distributor, C. Bruno has been known to market their own house brand.

BUCHANAN, ROY: See FRITZ BROS..

BUNKER: Weird Seventies brand name made somewhere in the Midwest. Design features included a detachable headstock with no tuning keys (they were found on the end of the body). A forerunner to Steinberger and other Eighties headless styles?

CAPITAL: House brand of Jenkins Music, a distributor from Kansas City. Most instruments seen with this brand are from the first half of the Twentieth Century, and many were made by Gibson.

CARRIVEAU: Unique, recent "eloustic" guitars, with design features of both electric and acoustic guitars. Made in Phoenix, Arizona.

CARSON ROBISON: A noted performer back in the Thirties who had his own brand name; most (if not all) instruments were made by Gibson.

CARVIN: Direct-order giant from Escondido, California. Manufactures and sells guitars, basses, amplifiers and sound reinforcement equipment. Carvins aren't particularly demand instruments in the used market, but they're very underrated.

CATALINA: House brand found on the headstock of Kay-made instruments from the Sixties. One vintage retailer stated that the name was also found on home hi-fi equipment from the same era, but he could not determine the retailer.

CHARVEL: Originally associated with Jackson, now appears to be exclusively imported instruments.

CHRIS: Budget/promotional line made by Jackson-Guldan, Inc. in Columbus, Ohio

COLLINGS: High-end flat-top and arch-top guitars hand-made by Bill Collings in Austin TX

CONKLIN: Incredibly wild-looking solidbody line, designed, of course, for rock & rollers. In 1989 this company re-located to Springfield, Missouri.

CORAL: An alternate (and fancier) brand name made by Danelectro in the late Sixties. Coral electric sitars sound like the Indian instruments for which they're named.

CROMWELL: A private label/house brand from around the Thirties; most (if not all) Cromwells were made by Gibson.

CURLEE, S.D.: Short-lived late Seventies brand that had commendable construction features, but somewhat plain looks. Another minus is the fact that most examples have no fret markers on their fretboards, which are usually maple. The name was later licensed to an overseas manufacturer, and such imports were very similar to domestic Curlees.

CUSTOM KRAFT: House brand name of St. Louis Music, a distributor. Instruments encountered have included ones made by Kay and Valco.

DANELECTRO: Probably the definitive example of cheezy Sixties-era instruments is the Sears Silvertone guitar that comes with an amplifier built into its carrying case, and this low-end favorite was made by Danelectro of New Jersey. All instruments made by this company were no-frills, durable pieces, and while much maligned during their time, they've nevertheless become somewhat sought-after due to the aforementioned cheezy appeal factor. **Eighty-five percent of the instruments made by Danelectro had the Sears "Silvertone" brand name**. The pickups of this brand were weird and wonderful: Their magnets and wiring were actually housed inside a **lipstick tube!!!** The bodies of lower-end Danelectros (such as the aforementioned Sears type) looked like solidbodies, but they actually had hollow chambers inside (the instruments were constructed of poplar and Masonite). Some Danelectro pieces such as the 12-string Bellzoukis and "Longhorn" basses are somewhat desirable. Danelectro had some association with Ampeg around the time of the Dan Armstrong "See Through" series, but they went out of business in the late Sixties.

D'ANGELICO: Legendary hand-made arch-top guitars from New York City; considered by many to be to guitars what Stradivarius instruments are to violins. Almost all are accounted for, so don't expect one to show up in a pawn shop unless it's **hot!**

D'AQUISTO: The author prefers to let Stan Jay, President of Mandolin Brothers, Ltd. (and writer of this book's Foreword) comment on D'Aquisto instruments:
"Originally he was the apprentice to John D'Angelico, but just as D'Angelico started making Gibson L-5 copies and gradually evolved his own designs, in the past 27 years James D'Aquisto, to an even greater extent, has done the same. At this time he is considered the dean of American archtop builders, whose work is aspired to but not equalled. His newest designs, including the "Classic" and the "Avant-Garde", are as thrilling to play, as exciting to hear, and as **different** from all that came before, as the original Gibson L-5 was, in 1923, as created by Lloyd Loar and Guy Hart, from the archtop roundhole Gibson guitars of the late Teens that preceded them. D'Aquisto's instruments are expensive, but they're as close to perfection in a guitar as any have come."

DEAN: Rock & roll solidbody guitars with unusual shapes and the distinctive Dean oversized "V" headstock. All Deans are now being made overseas; see chapter on name licensing for details.

DITSON: Founded in 1835 by a music publisher, Oliver Ditson, who ultimately founded the John Church Co. of Cincinnati, in 1860 and Lyon & Healy of Chicago in 1864. While other brands were also marketed by Ditson, some guitars had his own name. Other brands associated with Ditson included Bay State, Haynes and Tilton.

DOBRO: While "Dobro" is an acronym for "Dopyera Brothers", it has ultimately become a generic name for resonator guitars; that is, guitars with a large circular "hubcap"-like piece in the center of the body; the "resonator" is designed to enhance and amplify the sound of the instrument. Dobros are generally country instruments, and as such are considered "specialty" items (like mandolins and banjos) so they will not be addressed here.

DWIGHT: House brand belonging to a retail store; instruments included ones made by Gibson and Valco.

DYER BROS: Part of the Maurer, Euphonon and Prairie State group of instruments made by the Larson Brothers of Chicago during the first half of the 1900s.

EHLERS: High-priced flat tops made in Oregon City, Oregon

EPIPHONE: This name has been bounced around quite a bit when compared to other venerable American guitar brand names. The original Epiphones were New York-made, high quality instruments, and were primarily arch-tops. The name and manufacturing rights were sold to Gibson in the Fifties, and Epiphone guitars and basses were made in Kalamazoo, Michigan in the Gibson factory from 1959 through 1969. Gibson-made "Epis" are somewhat similar to Gibsons of the same era, with some differences in body styles and/or electronics. **Please note that most of the time that Gibson made Epiphones in Kalamazoo, they used the same serial numbering system as Gibson, so both brands can be at least partially dated in the same manner.** Beginning in the early Seventies, the Epiphone brand name was used on a line of imported instruments, and such guitars and basses are usually what are encountered in pawn shops.

EUPHONON: One of the brand names made by the Larson Brothers of Chicago during the first half of the Twentieth Century. Euphonons were a latter brand name for the Larsons, and most of them are 14-fret flat-tops that are relatively modern-looking. All Larson-made guitars are durable, although many have to be identified by an expert since they do not have logos on their headstocks.

FAVILLA: New York-made acoustics made from 1890-1973. Domestic-made Favillas have a family crest on the headstock while imported ones (1965-1973) have the **name only** in script on the headstock.

FENDER: See separate chapter.

FODERA: High-end instruments (usually basses) made in Brooklyn.

FRANKLIN: Fine, hand-made flat-tops from Washington state. Luthier Nick Kukich's creations are expensive, and are worth the price to owners. As of this writing, Franklin only has one authorized dealer in the U.S., Mandolin Brothers of Staten Island, NY.

FRITZ BROTHERS: Considered by some to be one of the best Fender Telecaster-style guitars currently being made. Originally conceived with the input of the late Roy Buchanan (a "player's player"), Fritz Brothers makes a solidbody "Roy Buchanan Bluesmaster" (with the guitar legend's name on the headstock), and semi-hollow "Deluxe" and "Custom" versions with the company name on the headstock. There **are**, however, some early versions that are semi-hollow with a "Roy Buchanan" headstock. Fritz Brothers is headquartered in Mobile, Alabama.

GALLAGHER: Small, hand-made guitar company located near Nashville.

GIBSON: See separate chapter.

G & L: The last venture of the late Leo Fender, who considered these instruments to be among the finest he'd ever made. Very underrated guitars and basses; they haven't yet achieved the demand status of Fenders.

GOWER: Nashville-based company in the Fifties and Sixties; reportedly made a decent instrument but now out of business.

GRAMMER: Another small, hand-made flat-top company from the Nashville area.

GRD: Unusual and rare solidbody electrics built in Vermont beginning in the Seventies.

GRETSCH: One of the "Cadillacs" of American guitars; often associated with Chet Atkins. Originally made in New York, they were known for their high-end arch-tops and arch-top electrics, including a variety of Chet Atkins endorsement models, the White Falcon, the Rally, the Viking and others. They also made solidbodies such as the Roc Jet, Duo Jet and the Silver Jet (which has a sparkle top). The Gretsch White Penguin is perhaps the rarest (and therefore the most valuable) of any American-made production guitar. The company underwent major changes in the Sixties and Seventies; production was moved to Arkansas in 1970, and two fires as well as several ownership changes eventually led to classic Gretsch styles being discontinued. In the late Seventies, some Gretsch instruments were made in Juarez, Mexico, and in late 1989 an overseas factory began to re-issue the classic Gretsch body styles, manufacturing them under name licensing.

GRUHN: Vintage authority George Gruhn has designed his own line of fine acoustic guitars. Some are domestic, some are imported.

GUILD: Another name that has undergone many ownership changes. Many vintage buffs feel that Guild arch-top and flat-top guitars are and have been professional quality instruments that have retained their value well. However, this writer has also heard some other folks malign Guilds as merely less-expensive copies of Gibsons. Guilds usually were less expensive than comparable Martin or Gibson models, but the "copy" stereotype is not a fair statement in the eyes of some knowledgeable guitar lovers. Guild electrics (particularly the solidbodies) have been through many changes and generally do not merit much interest. Arch-top electrics such as the X-500, on the other hand, are usually highly prized.

GURIAN: Underrated acoustic line built in New York City and New Hampshire from the early Sixties until 1982.

HAMER: Appearing in the Seventies, this Illinois company specializes in solid-body instruments with striking body styles and cosmetics, like Dean, B.C. Rich, etc.

HALLMARK: Short-lived California line made by an ex--Mosrite employee.

HARMONY: The "Big Daddy" of the Chicago-area manufacturers, rivaled only by Kay in terms of the volume of instruments produced. However, at one time Harmony was supposedly making more fretted instruments (including banjos, mandolins and ukeleles) **than all other U.S. manufacturers combined.** Naturally, this volume included a plethora of house brands for retailers and distributors. While Harmony instruments came in all styles, none of their instruments are particularly valuable, unless they have some very unusual feature, such as an arch-top electric from the Fifties that had **aluminum binding** around its edges (like a kitchen dinette from the same era)! While slightly nicer-looking than the no-frills Danelectro line, a Danelectro (or Sears Silvertone made by Danelectro) with the same comparable features as a Harmony would probably fetch more than a Harmony (or Harmony-made house brand) if both are in the same condition. Nevertheless, most Harmonys also have that retro-Sixties, cheezy appeal just like other cheapo lines from that time. As gargantuan as Harmony was, they still went out of business in the mid-Seventies, and the name has been licensed to a line of instruments made overseas.

HARPTONE: Relatively small manufacturer located in New Jersey from 1893 until the 1970s; at which time the brand name was sold to a Virginia company. Harptones are best known as having an innovative arched back on their acoustic instruments.

HAYNES: Associated with Ditson in the 1800s.

HERITAGE: After Gibson closed its plant in Kalamazoo, Michigan in the early Eighties, several former employees bought the plant and fixtures, and began producing the Heritage line of instruments. Obviously, they're not vintage items yet, but many guitar buffs feel that the quality and workmanship on these instruments is as fine, if not **better**, than comparable Gibson instruments; i.e., Heritage instruments aren't in demand now, but may prove to be a "sleeper"-type of collectible in the future.

HOLIDAY: House brand attributed to Montgomery Ward and Aldens; seen on instruments made by Danelectro, Harmony and Kay.

HOLZAPFEL & BEITEL: Baltimore-based manufacturer from around the turn of the century. Very little is known about them, but they also apparently made banjos and mandolins.

JACKSON: Texas-based, higher-priced solidbody rock & roll instruments. In the beginning, they were also associated with Wayne Charvel, but the Charvel line is now imported by Jackson.

JAY-G: Sub-brand seen on Kay-made instrument

JERRY JONES: One might speculate that this company is caught in a time warp. Jerry Jones has been a noted Nashville luthier for some time, making fine instruments for area players. However, in the late Eighties, when his company began making production instruments in larger volumes, they opted to market reproductions of **Danelectro** instruments! Such models include faithful reproductions of Longhorn basses, Electric Sitars and others. There are some refinements to Jerry Jones instruments to make them more reliable in their tuning, and a few other modern switches may be found, but all in all, Jerry Jones instruments are an admirable nostalgia brand, and they sound as unique as their Danelectro ancestors did.

JOHNSON, DEXTER: Fine handmade flat-tops, arch-tops, classical and flamenco guitars in Carmel-by-the-Sea, CA.

KALAMAZOO: The cheapest line ever made by Gibson. This brand dates all the way back to the Thirties, but is most often seen on a line of solidbody guitars and basses from the Sixties. Actually, "solidbody" is a slight misnomer here; the bodies of Sixties Kalamazoos were actually **molded chipboard!** They came in stock finishes (they had to!) and had bolt-on necks. They were somewhat Fender-ish in their appearance and used the same serial number system of the time as Gibsons and Gibson-made Epiphones. Some rare Sixties Kalamazoos with bodies made of solid wood instead of chipboard have been encountered, but they're not more valuable.

KAMICO: Kay sub-brand; acronym for KAy Musical Instrument COmpany.

KAPA: Budget line of solidbody guitars and basses made in Hayattsville, Maryland in the Sixties. Though not as oddball as another Maryland brand, Micro-Frets, Kapas were well-made. They appear to have had some imported parts such as pickups on them, and were apparently available through jobbers' catalogs. One of the more unusual Kapas encountered by the author is a 12-string electric guitar with a vibrato on it.

KAY: The other of Chicago's "Dynamic Duo" from the Sixties. Some Kay instruments go back to the Thirties (Kay Kraft guitars and mandolins, which had odd, almost spindle-shaped bodies), and some of their later models such as the Barney Kessel edition (which had a large, "keystone"-shaped headstock) were quite attractive. However, the definitive Kay-made guitar is a Plain-Jane single-pickup model with a plank-like body and all of **four** fret markers. There were varieties of body shapes and headstock shapes (as well as models with two and three pickups), and like Harmony, Kay made many house brand instruments. They went out of business in the late Sixties, and it appears that during the company's declining years, some imported parts such as pickups and hardware were used on domestic Kays. Like Harmony, the name is now licensed to an overseas manufacturer.

KOONTZ: Weird New Jersey-made guitars from the Sixties with odd gadgets built into them; relatively rare and desirable. Sam Koontz also designed guitars for Harptone and Standel.

KRAMER: Founded in 1976, Kramer quickly became a giant in the guitar business. They first made aluminum-neck models with wood inserts (Gary Kramer was a partner of Travis Bean's); these necks also were noted for their "tuning fork"-shaped headstocks and Ebonol fretboards (bowling ball material!!!) However, these earlier Kramers aren't particularly sought-after (some of them tend to be too neck-heavy). Kramer later switched to a more conventional construction style, and instruments have been made domestically as well as overseas under name licensing.

KUBICKI, PHILLIP: High-end "Factor" & "X-Factor" bass guitars.

KUSTOM: Back in the late Sixties, the folks that made those gaudy, tuck-and-roll Naugahyde-covered amplifiers made an abortive attempt to get into the guitar business as well. Their semi-hollow line featured one "cat's eye" f-hole, and the name was on a sticker inside the f-hole. While short-lived, these instruments aren't considered valuable; they're really more like curiosity items.

LA BAYE: Sixties oddity; the "2 x 4" guitar resembled exactly that. Made in Green Bay, Wisconsin.

LACEY, MARK: Los Angeles, CA - A maker of exquisite hand-made archtop jazz guitars, using restored vintage parts whenever possible.

LO PRINZI: Acoustic line made in New Jersey, beginning in 1972.

LYON & HEALY: Manufacturers of house brands and Washburn guitars from 1864-1927. Some instruments may also have had the Lyon & Healy name as well.

MAGNATONE: Sixties manufacturer of relatively undistinguished electric guitars. Some Magnatones may be imports.

MARATHON: House brand seen on Kay-made instrument.

MARTIN, C.F.:   The "ultimate" in mass-produced acoustic guitars and related instruments; in business since 1833. Serial numbers are easy to use when dating post-1898 instruments. Some Martin electrics exist, but they are not very valuable as they represent simply an abortive attempt by the folks in Nazareth, Pennsylvania to garner a bit of a market segment that they usually didn't cultivate, and their efforts seem to have been somewhat half-hearted. Please note that Martin's "Shenandoah" series is worth much less than regular Martins as they are made of foreign components that are merely put through their final assembly stages in the U.S. Regular Martins are, of course, valuable if in good or restorable condition, and should be treated with the respect they deserve.

MASTERTONE: Private label circa 1930s, most (if not all) were Gibson-made.

MAURER: Another of the underrated acoustic names made by the Larson brothers in the first half of the 1900s.

MAYBELL: Promotional brand circa 1930s; associated with Slingerland.

MERRILL: Aluminum-bodied instruments made around the turn of the century. Ahead of their time?

MESSENGER: Late Sixties line somewhat akin to Travis Beans and early Kramers (alloy necks). Made in San Francisco and not particularly desirable.

MICRO-FRETS: Maryland company in business from 1965 to 1972; made somewhat space age-looking instruments. This brand also had some unique innovations, such as a tunable nut!

MODULUS-GRAPHITE: Unusual and expensive instruments with graphite necks; best known for their use by members of the Grateful Dead.

MONTCLAIR: House brand; thought to be associated with Montgomery Ward. Seen on instruments by Kay and Premier.

MONTELEONE: Another current, exquisite hand-made line specializing in arch-tops, flat-tops and mandolins. This brand was the winner of Frets magazine's poll of luthiers (guitar-makers) for several years running. Generally considered to be close to the likes of D'Aquisto.

MONZA: See Premier.

MOSRITE: Surf's up! Mosrite guitars and basses are best known for their Sixties association with the instrumental group the Ventures. Luthier Semie Moseley (no relation to the author) has been in and out of several guitar-oriented ventures (no pun intended) throughout the years; he last surfaced in the late Eighties, making instruments in the bucolic community of Jonas Ridge, North Carolina.

MOSSMAN: Kansas-made acoustics; famous for their hand-crafting and fancy appointments; similar to Gallagher's reputation.

MUSIC MAN: Leo Fender's first post-Fender venture; makers of underrated guitars and basses. Not as highly sought-after as comparable guitars from better-known names.

NATIONAL: The oddball of the Chicago-area manufacturers; known for their unusual innovations in electric and acoustic instruments. Also associated with Dobro and Supro; the parent company of this line was Valco. Weird marketing ploys by National included map-shaped guitars, unusual location of controls, hidden pickups built into wooden bridges and "Gumby"-shaped headstocks. Went out of business in the late Sixties, and despite their eccentric features, National guitars generally don't fetch as much as better known brands of the same era.

NATIONAL RESO-PHONIC GUITAR CO.: A newer company founded by Donald L. Young, formerly of OMI/Dobro, primarily makers of very high quality replica wood-body prewar and '50's National resonator guitars. San Luis Obispo, CA

NOVA U.S.A.: Higher-end instruments made in Largo, Florida. Some exotic woods are used in certain Novas; one unique model is a flat-top acoustic-electric with a forearm bevel and a belly cut!

OAHU: Known primarily for its instructional publications regarding Hawaiian music, this company also marketed some instruments beginning around 1930; guitars were made by Harmony, Regal, Valco and Kay. Went out of business in 1985.

OLD KRAFTSMAN: Low-end brand name attributed to the Spiegel catalog, found on instruments made by Kay, Valco and Regal.

ORIOLE: House brand/private label from the first half of the Twentieth Century; Gibson made most (if not all) Oriole instruments.

ORPHEUM: Brand name applied to some Lange-made instruments from the Thirties until the early Sixties.

OVATION: Known primarily for their durable, professional round-backed acoustic guitars and acoustic-electric flat-tops.   Came into the market in the late Sixties and became very popular quite quickly.   Ovation has made some solidbody electrics from time to time that generally have not merited the serious interest of most collectors, but that attitude could be changing: One vintage authority consulted by the author in early 1991 feels that interest in Ovation solidbodies is picking up, and that such instruments may have been ahead of their time.

P'MICO: See Paramount.

PAGANI: Early 1900s line with Italian roots.

PARAMOUNT: The third name associated with William L. Lange instruments.   Actually, Lange made banjos, and some of their initial guitars were made by Martin (beginning in 1934).   Some Paramounts were very fancy instruments for their time, incorporating fancy woods and unusual soundhole construction.   Some Paramount-made instruments bore the name "P'Mico" on their headstocks; this was an acronym for Paramount Musical Instrument COmpany.

PEAVEY: As guitar and music technology exploded in the Eighties, Peavey attempted to become a well-priced, durable contender to compete with overseas manufacturers, and they succeeded in a tremendous way. Their guitars are excellent values as new instruments, so they don't fetch much as used ones. The T-60 guitar and T-40 bass could have been in the Eighties what Danelectro/Silvertones were in the Sixties; i.e., "everybody's first electric guitar". There are many varieties of Peavey instruments, none of which is worth too much when compared to other brands. However, this writer feels they are **very underrated** instruments, and that Peavey is a classic example of how American goods can still be well-made and competitive.

PEDULLA, M.V.:   High-end electric instruments, usually basses. A Pedulla with a bolt-on neck is worth much less, and was made by the company to hit a lower price point.

PENNCREST: House brand name for J.C. Penney. It appears that most of their domestic instruments were made by Kay.

PENSA-SUHR: Hand-made, high-end electrics; usually made on a special-order basis.

PERFORMANCE: Actually, Performance is more of a parts company, but some of their necks and bodies have this name on them. As a "parts" guitar, a Performance instrument might be a good utility instrument, but is it worth a lot???

PETILLO: Limited hand-made acoustics from Ocean, New Jersey. Some electrics are made as well, and the total number produced is probably less than twenty per year.

PRAIRIE STATE: Another line made by the Larson brothers in the first half of the Twentieth Century.

PREMIER: Relatively obscure line made in New York in the Fifties and Sixties. They tended to specialize in promotional instruments, and made several house brands, including Monza, Montclair (Montgomery Ward?) and Strad-O-Lin (Note: Most of these same brands also appeared on imported instruments as well!) One of the more unique cosmetic features of Premiers was a "scroll" effect on the upper cutaway, much like a mandolin. A subsequent series was the Bantam line, which were hollow-bodied instruments that resembled single-cutaway Gibson Les Pauls. In the case of Bantams and possibly some other latter day Premier-made instruments, imported parts were used.

RALEIGH: Same inexpensive line as Aloha.

RECORDING KING: House brand dating from the Thirties; instruments were made by Gibson and Regal.

REDONDO: House brand seen on the headstock of a budget Harmony-made instrument. The logo features a musical note poking into the first "O".

REGAL: Another Chicago promotional "big gun"; went out of business in 1954, but the name rights were acquired by Harmony, and the brand name is now found on a line of imported instruments.

REX: Somewhat of a mystery brand in that several vintage authorities have offered several opinions on its origin and history. Originally, Rex was a sub-brand of Gretsch in the early 1900s. One retailer opined that there was ultimately a connection to Regal, given the "royal" connotation to both names. However, the name has also been seen on a Kay-made promotional electric guitar from the Fifties, so who knows? It may have ended up as a house brand!

RICH, B.C.:   Another striking rock & roll solidbody line, somewhat like Dean and Hamer. B.C. Rich instruments are somewhat expensive, except for the models that are made overseas under name licensing.

RICKENBACKER: Credited with marketing the first electric guitar (a lap steel model), circa 1930. Rickenbackers are completely hand-made in California, and have held up considerably well in value over the years. Some of their finishes and body styles are unique. Many guitar buffs consider Rickenbackers to be to electric instruments what Martins are to acoustics; i.e., the definitive American instrument of its type. Surprisingly, "Ricks" are not out of line price-wise when compared to other American instruments being made today. They're not cheap, but they're not as extravagantly priced as brands such as Alembic, etc. In the late Eighties, there was actually a **waiting list** for Rickenbacker instruments, and the company has won some awards for the percentage of guitars and basses that they've exported (talk about reverse situations!). In some instances, the model of a Rickenbacker instrument will be printed on its truss rod cover.

ROBIN: Texas-made line of electric guitars and basses. Robins are somewhat underrated in some players' opinions, but they haven't been around long enough to merit any increase in value (and who knows to what extent that situation will change). Some early Robin models were Japanese-made.

ROGERS: House brand; instruments made by Vega. No relation to the drum manufacturer of the same name.

ROYALIST: House brand seen on headstock of a Kay-made arch-top acoustic-electric from the Fifties.

RUCK GUITARS: Expensive hand made Classical guitars by Robert Ruck in Poulsbo, WA.

SADOWSKY, ROGER: Known for instruments as well as parts (some guitars or basses may have a Sadowsky-made replacement neck, for instance). Complete Sadowsky instruments are relatively expensive but considered exceptional quality.

SAND GUITARS: Fine hand made thin-line classical electric, regular classical, and steel string flat-tops by Kirk Sand in Laguna Beach, CA.

SANTA CRUZ: Luxurious hand-made flat-top line; very expensive and made in Santa Cruz, California.

SAVANNAH: Brand name encountered on a budget flat-top; the words "Made in Ridgeland, South Carolina, U.S.A." were found inside the sound-hole. Ridgeland, S.C. is a few miles north of Savannah, Georgia.

SCHECTER: Higher-end instruments that are basically very good improvements on such instruments as Fender Stratocasters and Telecasters. However, they seem to sell for much less **proportionally** in the used market, given their higher original price. Like Performance and Sadowsky, Schecter also markets guitar replacement parts. Some Schecters are imported.

SCHOENBERG: Named for guitarist Eric Schoenberg; these instruments are partially assembled at the C.F. Martin factory. They are steel-string, fingerstyle guitars, and they reportedly utilize Martin serial numbers. The prime instrument is the "Soloist", and according to a Schoenberg ad, is individually Voiced®; such a procedure was done by Maine luthier Dana Bourgeois until sometime in 1990, when Bourgeois resigned from Schoenberg to develop a new line of acoustic guitars for Paul Reed Smith's company. Also in 1990, Schoenberg Guitars released its own fancy OM-45 Deluxe, a re-issue series totaling fourteen guitars; they were reproductions of the 1930 C.F. Martin OM-45 Deluxe, which also numbered fourteen instruments. Schoenberg Guitars is headquartered in Topsham, Maine.

SCHON: Relatively new solidbody line designed by Neil Schon, guitarist with such bands as Santana, Journey and Bad English. No real indication as of this writing as to whether or not they'll ultimately become desirable, but apparently Schon instruments and Fritz Bros.'s Roy Buchanan guitars are the first guitars to have a rock guitarist's name as the actual brand name, for whatever that's worth.

SCHWAB: Minneapolis company specializing in small "mini-guitars" and mandolins; most (if not all) are solidbody electrics.

SHANTI: Flat-tops handcrafted by Michael Hornick in Avery CA

SHERWOOD: House brand for Montgomery Ward.

SILVERTONE: Sears house brand.

SLINGERLAND: Known primarily for their drums and banjos, apparently this company also made some guitars in the Thirties. Most (if not all) were May Bell brand instruments.

SMECK, ROY: A noted multi-instrumentalist from the Twenties and Thirties, Smeck's name appeared on headstocks of instruments made by Gibson and Harmony; other manufacturers may have made Roy Smecks as well. When last heard from (in 1989), Smeck was ninety years old and was still teaching guitar in New York City.

SMITH, KEN: Very expensive instruments (almost exclusively bass guitars); this is one of the current manufacturers specializing in five-string and six-string basses.

SMITH, PAUL REED: A recent American success story; "P.R.S." instruments are made in Annapolis, Maryland. They're expensive and well worth the price to most professionals who purchase them. They are hand-made, using beautiful hardwoods. In most cases, a P.R.S. is "graded"; i.e., the fancier the construction, the higher the instrument is rated (and priced). One writer for a guitar publication has already opined that some of the early P.R.S. instruments will become collectibles in the future.

SPECTOR: Super-expensive instruments that became a favorite of many players in the Eighties. Distributed by Kramer, and like Kramer itself, some Spectors are imported, so be careful! Some original Spector instruments (the NS series) were designed by Ned Steinberger.

STANDEL: Harptone-made; short-lived line from the Sixties.

STAHL: From what can be determined, most of this Milwaukee firm's instruments were made by Larson Bros./Mauer group.

STELLING: Expensive flat-tops hand-made by Geoff Stelling in Afton VA.

ST. BLUES: Short-lived venture out of Memphis; their instruments were somewhat Fender-ish in appearance, and some models (if not all) utilized imported parts. Perhaps they were underrated, but they aren't particularly sought-after.

STELLA: The absolute nadir of American-made promotional instruments. Stella was a sub-brand of Chicago giant Harmony, and instruments had many easy-to-manufacture features, such as wood bridges that were set into the tops of flat-tops with screws (instead of being glued on). Most likely a Stella was the first guitar ever owned by anyone who was a teen during the Sixties. Like Harmony, the name is now found on a line of imported instruments.

STEINBERGER: The fretted music instrument industry was stunned in the late Seventies by the appearance of the Steinberger headless bass. Developed by industrial designer Ned Steinberger (who does not play a musical instrument), the basses were further unique in that their bodies and neck were made of space-age carbon/graphite/composite materials. Guitars soon followed the original basses, as did "hybrid" models with maple bodies (some of the wooden bodies were shaped like conventional solidbody guitars). All models remained headless until a new series called the "S" line appeared; it was the first Steinberger with a head-stock. Steinberger's success with a completely radical concept showed the music instrument industry not to discard upstart ideas out-of-hand, and not surprisingly, a plethora of Steinberger copies have appeared, as have headless instruments with tuning systems that are "licensed by Steinberger". Partners with Steinberger in his original venture included P. Robert Young (developer of the first fiberglass lifeboat), Stan Jay and Hap Kuffner. In 1987 the original founders sold Steinberger Sound Corporation to Gibson, but the instruments are still assembled in the Newburgh, New York factory, and the subsidiary is run autonomously.

STRAD-O-LIN: See Premier.

STROMBERG: In many players' opinions, this brand of arch-top is just about as legendary and desirable as D'Angelico. Many of Elmer Stromberg's creations were very large and very loud, and are highly prized.

STUDIO KING: Private label/house brand from the first half of the Twentieth Century; many instruments were made by Gibson.

SUPRO: Sub-brand of Valco; in many cases they were instruments that may have been closely related to Nationals, but without some cosmetic and/or electronic features.

TAYLOR: Relatively current and nicely-made acoustic line.

TILTON: Part of the Ditson group, with instruments dating back to the Civil War.

TONEMASTER: House brand seen on Valco-made instrument.

TRUETONE: House brand of Western Auto.

TURNER: A company founded by a former associate at Alembic, Rick Turner. Not as successful, from what can be determined, although Turners are greatly respected instruments and quite collectible.

VALCO: As previously noted, company name of the makers of National and Supro, as well as many house brands. Some guitars made have a Valco name on their headstocks.

VEGA: Underrated instruments made in Boston around the turn of the century until 1970, when they sold to Martin. Martin sold Vega in 1979 to Galaxy Trading Corp. where the name was poorly used by this Korean export line until 1989 when rights to the brand passed to Deering Banjo Company of Lemon Grove, CA.

VEILLETTE-CITRON: Exquisite but short-lived brand of guitars and basses; may ultimately become desirable due to their rarity and workmanship.

VALLEY ARTS: High-end, hand-crafted instruments made in Hollywood, CA

VELENO: Rare aluminum-bodied guitars from St. Petersburg, Florida. Sought-after primarily as a curiosity item. Their body style usually features two rounded, symmetrical cutaways and a "fish tail" headstock.

VIVI-TONE: Post-Gibson venture for their most famous designer, Lloyd Loar. Very odd and innovative features for their time (circa 1930).

WASHBURN: Lyon & Healy-made instruments from the late 1800s through about 1930. The name is now found on an imported line of acoustics and electronics. The brand derives from the middle name of George Washburn Lyon, co-founder of the original parent company (of Chicago), who loaned his name to the most elegant and prestigeous merchandise made by that firm.

WARMOUTH: Again, a parts manufacturer from which one can purchase all of the pieces necessary to make his/her own electric instrument.

WURLITZER: Another attempt by a keyboard company to get into fretted instrument business. Wurlitzers were reputed to have Kay-made bodies and German hardware. They were assembled in Elkhart, Indiana.

ZION: Hand-made solidbody electric line; relatively new. This brand seems to be a favorite of several Christian musicians (perhaps there's some connection with the name).

ZON: Also a relatively new line that primarily offers basses; somewhat expensive.

So there's a brief look at most of the American-made brands that are found in the new and used guitar market. If the reader is a pawn shop employee, this quick reference guide should be helpful in determining how much to loan on an instrument (if a shop even decides to make a loan). If the reader simply has an interest in a particular instrument he/she has encountered, perhaps this basic list of brands will encourage the reader to do further research.

This guide may not have been as extensive as some may wish, but it is as accurate as the information that has been researched allows. Particularly with brands that are noted as being discontinued and/or expensive, one should give serious consideration to having such instruments appraised by a reputable vintage instrument shop or authority. An appraisal would most likely furnish you with information that's more extensive than what's found in these capsule commentaries, **and** it could also give you a reasonable dollar figure of what such an instrument or instruments would fetch in the vintage/used guitar market.

FENDER INSTRUMENTS

Leo Fender's marketing of an electric solidbody Spanish guitar in 1950 turned the music world on its collective ear, and it hasn't been the same since. While other primitive solidbodies had appeared off and on since around 1930, the Fender "Broadcaster" was the first commercially successful one, spawning an infinite number of imitators. The "Broadcaster" became the "Telecaster" due to a legal dispute (for a short time no model name appeared on the headstock; these types made in the transition time between Broadcasters and Telecasters have been dubbed "Nocasters"!), and the "Tele" has remained relatively unchanged in over forty years except for refinements in tuning and electronics. A basic Telecaster still has a plank-like body, two single coil pickups, master volume and tone controls, a three-way toggle switch and a raucous, twangy sound.

Telecaster variations have included the following styles:

CUSTOM TELECASTER (1959-1970): Cosmetically fancier, with a sunburst finish and double-bound body.

TELECASTER THINLINE (1968-1979): A hollowed-out version with a single f-hole. First edition styles were made through January of 1972. Beginning in February of 1972, the Thinline had two larger, Fender humbucking pickups (with offset, "3+3" polepieces).

TELECASTER CUSTOM (1970-1981): This model had a Fender "3+3" humbucking pickup in the neck position, but a standard single coil unit from a bridge pickup. The controls also were different: separate volume and tone controls for each pickup, and the three-way toggle switch was found on the upper bout.

TELECASTER DELUXE (1973-1981): Somewhat slicker than other "Teles", featuring a headstock shaped like those found on Stratocasters or Precision basses, as well as a belly cut in back. Pickups were two Fender "3+3" humbuckers, and the control layout was the same as found on the Telecaster Custom.

Other styles have included Teles in paisley and floral finishes (1968-1970), Rosewood Telecasters (1969-1973), "Collectors Series" Telecasters such as the early Eighties Black & Gold Telecaster, and Telecaster Elites, which have active electronics. Vintage Re-Issue Teles have also been marketed; some are imported.

There have also been Telecaster basses, but these will be discussed in a separate section in this chapter on bass guitars.

ESQUIRE (1950-1970): Listed separately, although this instrument was basically a single-pickup Telecaster (bridge pickup only). The three-way toggle switch offered various tones instead of pickup selection. Like the Tele, the Esquire came in a Custom variant from 1959-1970. There were some very early two-pickup Fenders marketed under the "Esquire" name as well.

STRATOCASTER: The Fender Stratocaster has been the world's most popular guitar for many years. Appearing in 1954, the "Strat" has been through many variations, but it's still one hot-looking instrument, so imagine what the reaction was to this three-pickup, double-cutaway guitar back in the mid-Fifties! Andre Duchossoir has written a very fine handbook **on just this one guitar,** so to go into detail here would be somewhat redundant. However, between the models listed in Duchossoir's book and others, **plus** the types shown on a 1989 poster from Fender, the following variations of Stratocasters have either been made or are currently being manufactured:

Stratocaster (original)
25th Anniversary Stratocaster
Strat
Stratocaster Elite
The Strat
Walnut Strat
Gold Stratocaster
Contemporary Stratocaster (import)
American Standard Stratocaster
Vintage Re-Issue Stratocaster (domestic)
Vintage Re-Issue Stratocaster (import)
HLE Gold Stratocaster
Stratocaster XII
Strat Plus
Squier Stratocaster (import)
Bullet Stratocaster (usually imported)

It's easy to see why so much confusion exists concerning Stratocasters; Fender is constantly bringing out new colors in limited quantities, or some new limited edition will pop up on a regular basis. However, there have been some oddball, one-off Strats that have been produced, including a clear Lucite model in 1957, and a paisley Stratocaster in the late Seventies (both are accounted for, and the paisley version is now being made in Japan and imported to the U.S.). Duchossoir's book is the definitive guide to the world's most popular guitar, and contains not only valuable historical information, but construction and design information as well.

DUO-SONIC (1955-1980): Budget-priced two-pickup model in stock finishes.

MUSICMASTER (1955-1980): Single-pickup version of the Duo-Sonic, although a two pickup "Musicmaster II" appeared in the mid-Seventies, differing from the then-current "Duo-Sonic II" in that the Duo-Sonic II had an extra set of controls on its upper half.

JAZZMASTER (late 1957/early 1958-1980): The first Fender guitar to feature an "offset waist" design; i.e. the "pinched" or "waist" areas on the guitar body were not symmetrical (as found on previous Fender instruments); this design gave greater comfort and balance to a player. The Jazzmaster had several other innovative features such as a locking vibrato arm that prevented de-tuning in case a string broke, and **two** sets of controls, which meant switching from rhythm status to play a lead was as simple as flicking a switch once volume and tone were pre-set.

JAGUAR (1960-1975): Essentially a Jazzmaster with a shorter scale and different electronics. Curiously, Jaguars and Jazzmasters were higher-priced than Stratocasters during their time, but they aren't much in demand in the vintage market, whereas vintage Strats usually command top dollar if they're in nice shape. This could, of course, be subject to change.

MUSTANG (1964-1981): Essentially a Duo-Sonic with a vibrato arm.

ELECTRIC XII (1965-1969): Fender's 12-string electric had its twelve tuning keys located on what was dubbed a "hockey stick" headstock. It had two "split" pickups, and was the first Fender guitar to have such a pickup configuration (although the Precision Bass had had a split pickup since 1957; see this chapter's section on bass guitars).

CORONADO (1966-1970): The thinline, f-hole Coronado series was apparently a turkey for Fender. They came in the following configurations: Coronado I (single pickup guitar), Coronado II (double pickup guitar), Coronado XII (12 string, two pickups), Coronado Bass I (single pickup) and Coronado Bass II (two pickups). In 1966, a special "Coronado Wildwood" series appeared, featuring unique colored instruments that were made from **trees that had dye injected into them while they were still growing!** The Wildwood concept also appeared in some Fender acoustic guitars during the same period. Some instruments in the Coronado series were re-dubbed "Antiguas" when they were marketed in Fender's "Antigua" finish (an off-white to grey sunburst; this finish is also found on other Fender instruments).

were re-dubbed "Antiguas" when they were marketed in Fender's "Antigua" finish (an off-white to grey sunburst; this finish is also found on other Fender instruments).

BRONCO (1967-1980): Single-pickup budget guitar (like a Musicmaster) with a vibrato; the solitary pickup was more towards the bridge than the one on a single-pickup Musicmaster. Originally marketed with a matching amplifier as a set.

MONTEGO (1968-1974): Arch-top jazz guitars, unique cosmetically in that they had three-on-side tuners. The Montego I had one pickup and the Montego II had two.

LTD (1968-1974): Hand-carved version of the Montego. Very exquisite and very expensive.

MUSICLANDER/SWINGER/ARROW (1969): A rare and unusual single pickup guitar made from parts of other instruments. While it is suspected that most of the parts were from promotional guitars such as Duo-Sonics, Mustangs and Musicmasters, the bodies were apparently crafted from leftover Bass V bodies. One publication reports that body routing found under the pickguard was for one split pickup (which the Bass V had). The Musiclander had a headstock that was pointed with six-on-a-side tuners; this is the origin of the "Arrow" nickname. However, "Swinger" was the only name that ever appeared on the headstock beside the Fender logo.

CUSTOM (1969): Another attempt to use up old parts; this time the hybrid was made from Electric XII bodies and neck as well as Electric XII electronics. The bodies were cut to a slightly different shape, and the hockey stick headstock had three-on-a-side tuners. A Mustang-type vibrato was also added. Also rare, but also ugly.

STARCASTER (1976-1980): Fender's attempt at a thinline semi-solid instrument. The Starcaster of course resembled the Gibson ES-335 and related models, as it had a centered block of wood inside its thinline hollow body. Unique features included offset double cutaways, a slightly different six-on-a-side headstock style, and a master volume control (total of five knobs). Pickups were two Fender 3 + 3 humbuckers.

LEAD (Early Eighties): Comprised of the Lead I, II and III, this was apparently an attempt at a budget Strat that didn't sell. The body was slightly down-sized, and there was some confusion regarding the controls among potential players. These may have been underrated, but they're not sought by guitar enthusiasts.

ACOUSTIC INSTRUMENTS: Fender's first venture into acoustics came about in the Sixties. All of the instruments had the classic six-on-a-side Fender headstock (except 12-string models, which of course had a hockey stick headstock). They were not very fancy but neither were they budget instruments (at one point, however, Harmony of Chicago made some Fender flat-tops; these have three-on-a-side tuners and a single-color Fender logo, usually white). Fender-made acoustics included the following models:

Kingman	Redondo
Concert	Palomino
Malibu	Shenandoah 12-string
Newporter	Villager 12-string

As previously noted, the "Wildwood" wood dye treatment was also found in Fender's acoustic division. A guitar known as the Wildwood came in several colors, and was similar to the Kingman. There were also some other rare domestic Fender acoustics that were made in small quantities; the author once encountered an unusual Fender "King", which resembled a Kingman, except it had a clear pickguard and "checkered" binding (see Photo Section). Fender got out of the domestic acoustic market around 1971, and subsequent Fender acoustics have all been imported.

BASS GUITARS

Fender's bass guitars deserve their own separate listing. For all of the controversy regarding who developed or invented the solidbody electric guitar, there doesn't seem to be any argument that the Fender company invented the solidbody bass. The Precision bass was announced and marketed in 1951, and is still the world's most popular bass guitar. In face, for some years the term "Fender bass" was a **generic name for any solidbody bass by any manufacturer** (other marketing examples include Kleenex, Band-Aid, etc.)!

The original Precision was revolutionary, but also relatively primitive when compared to some brands and models made today. It had a slab-type body and a single-coil pickup under a chrome cover. A chrome cover also was placed over the bridge/tailpiece, and the bass had a volume and tone control.

The body was contoured beginning in 1954, and in 1957 a split humbucking-type pickup replaced the single-coil unit. With the exception of minor refinements (usually to hardware or cosmetics) the basic Precision has been unchanged since then.

Like Stratocasters and Telecasters, Precisions have been introduced in several variants over the years. Naturally, Vintage Re-Issues have been marketed, but among the other editions are the Precision Bass Special (active electronics), Precision Elite (two split pickups, active electronics), Walnut Precision Bass and others.

JAZZ BASS (1960-Present): The second bass guitar introduced by Fender was quite different from the Precision. The Jazz bass had two single coil pickups, a slimmer neck and a contoured, offset waist body like the Jazzmaster and Jaguar. The original Jazz models had two control knobs which were actually volume and tone controls for each pickup mounted in concentric configuration, with the volume control inside and the tone control outside (the radios in most automobiles are set up like this, as were some Danelectro instruments). This control configuration is known as the "stack knob" or "stack pot" type and was only in production for about a year before Fender switched to two volume pots and one master tone pot; the tone knob was smaller.

Some Jazz variants include the early Eighties Gold Jazz and a Vintage Re-Issue that has stack pots.

BASS VI (1962-1975): "Baritone guitar" with a 30" scale. Offset waist body style; looked somewhat like a three-pickup Jaguar. It even had a vibrato!

BASS V (1965-1971): Split-pickup, full scale bass with an extra, higher pitched string designed to be tuned to "C". The neck joined the body at the 15th fret; the line of thinking here was that the extra string meant that a player should not have to go as high on the neck to get to higher notes. Ahead of its time in many ways.

MUSTANG BASS (1966-1981): The first short-scale bass marketed by Fender had a single split pickup (oval-shaped sections.

TELECASTER BASS (1968-1979): The first edition of the Telecaster bass was for all intents and purposes a re-issue of the original 1951 plank-like Precision. In 1972 a Fender "2+2" bass humbucking pickup replaced the original pickup; the humbucker was located closer to the neck. About the only variants of the Tele bass that were marketed were paisley and floral editions that were produced around the same time as paisley and floral Telecaster guitars.

MUSICMASTER BASS (1971-1982): The other short-scale Fender bass had one single-coil pickup and was very similar to the Mustang bass.

Bass guitars that were introduced as part of an entire series (Coronado, Antigua) have already been cited; they were all full scale instruments.

There are some cosmetic factors that may make some Fender instruments more desirable and valuable. Gold hardware instead of chrome is a big plus, as are custom colors instead of stock finishes.

Many times when older Fender instruments are being discussed, the term "pre-CBS" will be heard. CBS bought Fender Musical Instruments in 1965 (and sold it back to a consortium consisting of Fender employees, a bank, an investment firm from Chicago and musician Tommy Tedesco in 1985). "Pre-CBS" instruments made prior to the 1965 sale have a certain "aura" about them that makes them more desirable.

LOGOS
Logos found on Fender headstocks have varied with the times. The original logo is sometimes called "spaghetti" or "pre-CBS" logo; the latter designation is technically erroneous, as Fender began using their current script logo in 1960. However, some "spaghetti" logos were used on certain instruments through 1967, and such logos are also found on Vintage Re-Issue Fenders. "Spaghetti" logos are gold or silver with a black outline.

Most of the earlier current script logos are gold with a black outline, and are popularly referred to as "transition" logos, as yet another nod to the CBS takeover. Subsequent logos were black (most of the time with a gold outline) until around 1980, when most models began sporting a silver logo with a black outline; some Fenders may have a black logo with a silver outline.

A complication involving Fender instruments involved the fact that many times whenever a counterfeit or forgery is encountered, the style and/or color of the headstock logo can immediately alert someone that an instrument is a phony. This situation has not been helped by the fact that some folks sell pseudo-Fender "spaghetti" logo **decals** for about two dollars each!

DATING FENDERS: A SIMPLE PROCEDURE

A simple way of determining when a particular Fender most likely was made is to detach the neck and examine both the end of the neck and the neck slot; many times a date will be penciled or stamped there (the neck dating procedure was discontinued by Fender from about 1973 to 1982). Other body cavities, such as areas routed for pickup placement, may also have dates in them. In fact, some pickups themselves are dated, but most of the time someone should not have to go to that much trouble in order to date a Fender guitar or bass.

Some late entries in Fender's lineup, such as the H.M. Strat and the Precision Plus, have been purposely omitted. They are current production models as of this writing with newer, perhaps more innovative features, but instruments these days seem to be more technology-oriented and "over-refined", and perhaps the classic sound can only be found in classic instruments. Such high-spec guitars and basses may be great for utility purposes, but to what extent they have that much "soul" is a subject of intense debate among many musicians.

With the death of Leo Fender in March 1991 Strat and Tele prices started to climb again. Stan Jay says, "Rumors of the death of Leo Fender began circulating at the Greater Southwest Guitar Show in Dallas. Even at that show visitors and dealers began buying up Fender instruments they might not have formerly considered purchasing, presumably on the speculation that Fender prices would suddenly become higher. Although some might say "How odd that Leo Fender's death would cause the market to change - he wasn't making any Fender brand guitars, and certainly wasn't making any pre-CBS guitars.' you have to remember that, in the stock market, prices rise and fall on the basis of even the most benign rumors. Whether or not the changes in buyer perception brought about by Mr. Fender's passing will genuinely affect the value of vintage and used Fenders still remains to be seen."

NOTE: The following names and terms for instruments are registered trademarks of Fender Musical Instrument Company:

STRATOCASTER	STRAT	STRAT PLUS
TELECASTER	TELE	TELECASTER CUSTOM
TELECASTER DELUXE	CUSTOM TELECASTER	PRECISION BASS
P-BASS	P-BASS ELITE	CORONADO
ANTIGUA	JASS BASS	J-BASS
MUSTANG	MUSTANG BASS	MUSICMASTER
MUSICMASTER BASS	MUSICLANDER	SWINGER
BASS V	BASS VI	ELITE SERIES
ESQUIRE	STARCASTER	SQUIER
BULLET	DUO-SONIC	JAZZMASTER
JAGUAR	ELECTRIC XII	MONTEGO
BRONCO	LTD	CUSTOM
TELECASTER	KINGMAN	CONCERT
MALIBU	NEWPORTER	REDONDO
PALOMINO	SHENANDOAH	VILLAGER

GIBSON INSTRUMENTS

What hath Orville Gibson (1856-1918) wrought? The name Gibson has been popular among American fretted instruments since the late 1800s, and the company has been credited with introducing and/or patenting some of the most unique, revolutionary and ultimately popular innovations in the guitar industry.

Gibson has been through several ownership changes over the decades, and some guitar enthusiasts have complained that such changes have contributed to sometimes inferior products and/or lousy marketing when compared to earlier Gibson instruments. Nevertheless, Gibson still offers a player the widest selection of instruments at an extremely broad pricing structure when compared to other U.S. manufacturers.

Originally manufactured in Kalamazoo, Michigan, most Gibson instruments are now being made in Nashville, Tennessee. The company opened the second plant in Nashville in the mid-Seventies, with the intention of manufacturing only solidbody instruments there; ultimately the Michigan plant closed and the entire operation was moved to Nashville. In 1989, Gibson began manufacturing acoustic instruments in Montana.

Once again, other publications that are already in print offer much more detailed information about Gibson instruments than what will be found here, so consider this chapter (like the one on Fender) to be an overview of the brand name.

Naturally, almost any older Gibson instrument that is in good shape will be relatively desirable and valuable, although certain models may not fetch as much as some may think. Gibson is such a diverse line that for brevity's sake, the following capsule commentaries will be quite general.

Any Gibson instrument that is from the "Lloyd Loar" period (1919-1924) would automatically merit interest; Loar was a pioneer of guitar "research and development" and some Gibson instruments have his signature on their inside label. Loar departed Gibson to form Vivi-Tone after five years with the Kalamazoo firm.

Earlier Gibsons included guitars that had "L" and "O" prefixes. The L-5 (designed by Loar) is still in production, as is the Super 400 (introduced in 1935) and the Super Jumbo 200/J-200 flat-top guitar; the L-5 and the Super 400 have electric variants. All of them **were and are** considered high-end instruments.

There were, of course, many other acoustic archtops and flat-tops that were introduced and discontinued by Gibson over the decades; prefixes included "J" and "B".

Gibson's first electric Spanish guitar was the ES-150, introduced in 1937. Although other electric guitars had been appearing in the Thirties, Gibson was so large that their introduction of such a guitar meant that the concept was given more credibility; i.e., when Gibson endorsed an idea, musicians paid more attention! Other electric guitars soon followed, as did electric versions of acoustic models.

Gibson entered the solidbody electric guitar field in 1952, with the introduction of the first Les Paul model, and their Electric Bass (the capitalized letters are intentional, as that was the name given to the instrument) appeared in 1953. While following the groundbreaking efforts of Fender in both categories, Gibson nevertheless sought to carve out their own market share with these new guitar innovations, and was particularly successful with Les Pauls; the evolution of the Les Paul series as well as electric basses will be documented later in this chapter.

Gibson didn't play "follow the leader" with Fender during the Fifties, however. Under the guidance of Ted McCarty, the 1950s saw the development, patenting and marketing of such now-standard guitar parts as humbucking pickups, stop/bar-type tailpieces, and tunable bridge saddles (the terms "humbucking" and "tune-a-matic" were original names as stated in Gibson patents; however, they have since become **generic** terminology with the guitar industry. As previously noted, such was also the case for a time with the "Fender bass").

The semi-solid thinline guitar was another child of the Fifties; the ES-335 was introduced in 1958. That same year saw the introduction of two "Modernistic" guitars, the Explorer and Flying V. Although unsuccessful back then, first series Explorers and Flying Vs fetch extraordinary prices in the vintage market due to their rarity.

The original single-cutaway Les Paul was discontinued around 1960 in favor of a double-cutaway instrument; the cutaways were nearly symmetrical and sharp-pointed. Dubbed as Les Pauls for a short time, they were re-named SGs (for Solid Guitar) and were Gibson's mainline solidbody throughout the Sixties. Original style Les Pauls came back around 1968 with the introduction of the Les Paul Deluxe, which had mini-humbuckers. The Sixties also saw the rise and fall of two styles of Gibson Firebirds.

The Seventies were a bit more complicated, with Gibson's management not only continuing to market their bread-and-butter acoustics and electrics, but introducing new concepts (at least for Gibson) such as electric guitars with bolt-on necks (excepting the Kalamazoo sub-brand from the Sixties), and electric guitars with 24-fret necks (the first was the L6-S). The oft-maligned RD series of instruments also appeared, in 1977. Most of these Seventies innovative ideas were unsuccessful and the instruments most likely will not be very desirable in the future, even if they were "underrated" and/or "ahead of their time".

It seems that quite possibly the same could be said for Gibson in the Eighties as well; Gibson's "old stand-bys" continued to be responsible for the bulk of their business, and most of their innovations in that decade as well didn't go over; a definitive example would be the Steinberger-designed "20/20" bass, which had active circuitry.

Like Fender, Gibson was shrewd enough to begin marketing certain re-issues of some of their classic instruments, but in some cases certain re-issues are cosmetically different from their ancestors. Remaining faithful to the construction of an original model seemed to "get back on track" for Gibson in the mid-Eighties, although Gibson "re-issues" date back to the late Sixties.

Gibson's acoustics and electric acoustics have experienced few changes over the years, except for a few models being dropped or added, or improved parts being introduced. Some of their most popular and/or noteworthy instruments include:

HUMMINGBIRD and DOVE: Two flat-top acoustics that usually have their respective namesakes embossed on their pickguards. Both have "double parallelogram" fret markers; sometimes block markers are seen.

ES-125: Electric acoustic available in many versions, including full-depth or thinline body styles, one or two pickup models, and bodies with no cutaways or a single Florentine (pointed) cutaway. Naturally, combinations of the above features could be found on one instrument, and a 3/4 scale guitar was also made (single pickup, no cutaway). The ES-125 was Gibson's "workhorse" for years.

ES-175: Upgrade, jazz-oriented electric archtop with double parallelogram fret markers and a Florentine cutaway. Like the ES-125, it also has been available with one or two pickups and in a full-depth or thinline body style.

EVERLY BROTHERS: Flat-top model with large pickguards (on each half of instrument) and star-shaped fret markers.

ES-5: Introduced in 1949, this was the first electric guitar marketed with three pickups. A later version offered a four-way toggle switch (one pickup at a time or all three); this incarnation was known as the "Switchmaster".

BYRDLAND: A thinline two-pickup electric introduced circa 1955, named after two guitarists of note at that time, Bill BYRD and Hank GarLAND. Florentine or Venetian (rounded) cutaway.

ES-295: An all-gold version of the ES-175 with two creme P-90 pickups. Matched the original Les Paul solidbody guitar; both introduced in 1952.

ES-225: Gibson's first thinline electric, introduced in 1955. Replaced by the ES-125, which was practically the same instrument.

As for semi-solid thinline electrics, this series of Gibson instruments has remained relatively unchanged since the ES-335 was introduced in 1958. Its "upgrade cousins" have included the ES-345 and ES-355; most of the step-up models feature stereo wiring and a "Varitone" tone switch.

Other thinline semi-solids manufactured by Gibson over the years have included the ES-347 (different wiring), the ES-325 (mini-humbucking pickups) and the rare ES-320 (early Seventies beginner's thinline with two small, Melody Maker-type single coil pickups; it is not considered too valuable or desirable).

Mention should also be made at this point of two other models that resembled the thinline semi-solid "300" series. The super-rare Crest was made circa 1969-71. It had an all-rosewood body and mini-humbucking pickups. The promotional ES-330 had one or two P-90 pickups. While both of these models resembled other "300 thinliners", **neither the Crest (which is highly prized) nor the ES-330 had an internal wood block inside their bodies.**

SOLID-BODY GUITARS and BASSES

Gibson's solidbody lineup had undergone a plethora of changes since the original Les Paul model was introduced in 1952. For the sake of brevity, we will take a look at only the more popular models (then **and** now) in detail, and will generally list most of the styles that weren't successful when they were introduced (and as a general rule, the same instruments aren't highly sought today, but there are some notable exceptions).

THE FIFTIES:
SINGLE-CUTAWAY LES PAULS and "MODERNISTIC" GUITARS

The original Les Paul was a gold-top, single cutaway, two-pickup model with a large "trapeze" bridge/tailpiece. This was soon changed to a stop/bar bridge/tailpiece, and the instrument went through several other variations in the Fifties. Chronologically, the changes included a separate stop/bar tailpiece and tune-a-matic bridge (1955), humbucking pickups (1957), and a "Cherry Sunburst" finish (red and yellow) that showed off the maple top underneath; if late Fifties Cherry Sunburst Les Pauls have a lot of "flame maple" on their tops, they fetch unbelievable prices in the vintage market if they are in good condition.

Standard features on all Fifties "Les Paul Standard" guitars (the model took this name as other Les Paul models were introduced) included pearloid (celluloid) trapezoid-shaped fret markers beginning on the third fret, separate volume and tone pots for each pickup and a three-way toggle switch on the upper bout.

Three other Les Paul models appeared in the Fifties:

LES PAUL CUSTOM (1954): A classy, upgrade instrument, with an ebony fretboard and mother of pearl block-shaped fret markers beginning on the first fret. Also took on humbucking pickups around the same time as the Standard, but Customs got **three** humbucking pickups instead of two. Some Les Paul Customs from the late Fifties **do** exist with two humbucking pickups, however. All production Les Paul Customs from this era were black with gold hardware, and they were nicknamed "Black Beauty" or "Fretless Wonder"; the latter connotation was due to their smooth, fast playing. Les Paul Customs had a separate stop/bar tailpiece and tune-a-matic bridge when they were introduced, and they maintained this configuration.

LES PAUL JR. (1954): On the opposite end, the Les Paul Jr. was introduced the same year as the Custom. It had a single P-90 pickup and a combination bridge/tailpiece in a stop/bar style. Their original finish was a standard brown sunburst similar to that found on many Gibson flat-tops and arch-tops of the time. The fretboard had dot markers, and the Gibson logo on the headstock was screen-printed in gold (the Standard and Custom had pearl logos).

From its introduction, the Les Paul Jr. was also made in a light, natural finish known as "limed mahogany"; this color was apparently nicknamed as the "TV" finish, since it showed up better when musicians performed on television. (Most Fifties TV sets were monochrome/"black-and-white"). In 1957 Gibson officially named their Les Paul Jr. in a limed mahogany finish as the "Les Paul TV".

LES PAUL SPECIAL (1955): A two-pickup version of the Les Paul Jr. with some minor cosmetic differences, such as a pearl headstock logo (like other two-pickup Les Pauls). The Special was introduced in the aforementioned "limed mahogany" or "TV" finish; apparently no production Specials were finished in sunburst. Like the Jr., the Special had a one-piece bridge/tailpiece.

In the late Fifties, all three "dot neck" Les Pauls (Jr., TV and Special) underwent several changes. In 1958, the Jr. and TV were re-styled with an offset, double-cutaway body, which made for easier playing access on the higher registers. Also, the Jr.'s sunburst finish was replaced by a cherry finish. The Special followed suit in 1959, although it remained available in a TV finish as well as a new cherry finish. Curiously, the limed mahogany finish on the Les Paul Special was never referred to by Gibson as a "TV" finish; this designation was only applied to the light-finished Les Paul Jr., which became the Les Paul TV.

Certain unusual Les Paul Jr. and Les Paul Special variants were made during the Fifties. These included 3/4 scale Jr.s and Specials as well as four-string "tenor" or "plectrum" guitars using a Les Paul Special as the foundation.

Over the decades, the single-cutaway Les Paul style has been made in many variants with many catchy names. Not only have quite a few re-issues been marketed (although as previously noted, some Gibson re-issues are not exact reproductions of their predecessors), other Les Pauls with different electronic and/or cosmetic features have come and gone. Among these different Les Paul editions have been:

LES PAUL DELUXE: Marketed in the late Sixties and made through the early Eighties; basically a Les Paul Standard with mini-humbuckers. Inspired by the success of the Deluxe, Gibson issued a limited edition Standard (with full-size humbuckers) in a "Tobacco Sunburst" finish around 1974, and ultimately the Les Paul Standard came back into full production.

LES PAUL RECORDING: Designed somewhat for what its name implies, this version had lots of tone gizmos and large, oval-shaped low impedance pickups. The Les Paul Recording had been preceded by the LES PAUL PERSONAL and the LES PAUL PROFESSIONAL, which also had low impedance pickups, but none of these fancier models gained much acceptance among players. There were also basses with low impedance pickups; among these were the LES PAUL PROFESSIONAL BASS and the LES PAUL TRIUMPH.

LES PAUL PRO: Late Seventies through early Eighties; had two creme P-90 pickups plus an ebony fretboard.

LES PAUL ARTIST: Introduced in 1979 with "Artist" active circuitry, as found in the RD series of instruments.

LES PAUL ARTISAN: Mid-to-late Seventies style with fancy headstock and fretboard inlay; came in two- and three-pickup versions.

THE LES PAUL: Super-rare, super-high-priced edition in natural finish with striking "flame maple" top, back and neck. The parts on this type that normally would have been plastic (pickguard, controls, etc.) were instead made of **wood**!

LES PAUL CUSTOM LITE: A thinner-bodied Custom that weighs two pounds less; also has slightly different controls.

LES PAUL STUDIO: Somewhat lower-priced with humbucking pickups, and an unbound neck.

THE PAUL: Late Seventies budget instrument; see this chapter's section on promotional Gibsons.

There are a few other editions of single-cutaway Les Pauls as well, and there were also Les Pauls in body styles other than the classic single-cutaway style.

The change in the decade also meant changes were in the works concerning Gibson's solidbody guitar line. The budget-priced Melody Maker was introduced in 1959 (more about it later), and in 1960 Gibson opted to revamp their mainline solidbody series. The Les Paul Jr., TV and Special became the SG Jr., SG TV and SG Special, and maintained their offset, double-cutaway style. Ultimately the entire line of what had been called Les Paul guitars was restyled into the SG line.

Before the Fifties are left behind, special mention needs to be made of the rare "Modernistic" guitars. Gibson patented three futuristic body styles in the mid-Fifties, and two of them were actually produced. Their bodies were made of African limba wood; the name of the wood in Gibson promotional materials was "Korina".

FLYING V: Most likely, 120 original Flying Vs were made (in three batches of 40) in 1958 and 1959. The name of the guitar of course describes its shape, and its headstock resembled an arrowhead. Original Fifties Vs had strings that loaded from the rear of the body (in other words, no tailpiece, as was the case with Fender

Telecasters and Stratocasters), two humbucking pickups and gold hardware. Its "Natural" finish is golden-colored.

Some original Flying Vs were shipped as late as 1963, according to Gibson records; some of these latter guitars may have had some differences in cosmetics, such as different colored pickguards and/or hardware.

EXPLORER: Following close on the heels of the Flying V's introduction, Gibson marketed the bizarre, "zig-zag"-shaped Explorer (the name was possibly a nod to America's first artificial satellite, successfully launched in early 1958). Sporting an incredibly unbalanced set of cutaways (at least **visually**), the Explorer was nevertheless comfortable and balanced when played (as was the Flying V, for that matter). The earliest versions had a V-shaped headstock (which may have inspired Dean a couple of decades later), but most Explorers had a six-on-a-side headstock (the first Gibsons to have such). Much confusion exists as to the exact number of Explorers produced, as Gibson's shipping records refer to a total of 22 "Mod." guitars being shipped in 1958 and 1959 that may have been Explorers **and/or prototype guitars** (including Modernes? See next paragraph). According to a Gibson Vice-President, most of the employees involved with Fifties Explorers feel that around 40 were made.

The patent for instrument body styles filed by Gibson in 1957 includes a third shape, that of the "Moderne". One half of its body resembles a Flying V while the other half is smaller. Its headstock shape looks like some kind of putty knife; overall the instrument's silhouette resembles a Praying Mantis! Supposedly this guitar made it all the way through the prototype stage (even more futuristic shapes were designed but discarded) but Gibson opted not to market the "Moderne". If a prototype Moderne from 1958 exists and could be located, it would immediately set off a bidding war between the world's most affluent guitar collectors. This ugly-as-sin instrument has been dubbed "The Holy Grail" by guitar buffs.

Gibson has made many varieties of Flying Vs and Explorers through the years, beginning in 1967 with a Flying V re-issue. Some of the variants are not too popular among vintage buffs; the late Seventies "V-2" (laminated and sculpted body, "boomerang"-shaped pickups) is an example of a "bow-wow".

The Moderne became a re-issue (of a guitar that may have never existed!) in 1982, and other series of Modernes have been made since then.

Even though the original "Modernistic" guitars were commercial failures in their time, they have ultimately attained the highest rank of respectability as collector's pieces. Considering the shapes of many solidbody guitars being made these days, these late Fifties futuristic instruments may indeed have been ahead of their time!

THE SIXTIES:
SGs AND FIREBIRDS

As previously noted, Gibson began the transition from the single-cutaway Les Paul body style to a double-cutaway style with the revamping of the Les Paul Jr., Les Paul TV and the Les Paul Special in the late Fifties; these were eventually renamed the SG Jr., SG TV, and SG Special.

The offset, rounded double-cutaway body style was somewhat short-lived, however; the entire line of Gibson solidbody instruments was re-styled in late 1960 and introduced in 1961 in a new, double-cutaway body style with sharp, pointed cutaways that were nearly symmetrical. This look of course became known as the classic SG body style, and for a brief period even some of these body styles sported a Les Paul name; within the vintage market these are known as "SG/Les Pauls", and perhaps the most famous example of one is the psychedelic-painted instrument used by Eric Clapton during his stint with Cream.

For the most part, Sixties models of SGs conformed to their Fifties Les Paul counterparts when it came to electronics, fretboard inlay, etc. For example, the SG Custom had three pickups, block markers beginning on the first fret, etc. However, the SG Custom generally was produced in **white**, compared to the Les Paul Custom's black finish. Other finishes on specific SG models were as follows:

SG STANDARD: Cherry finish was standard; some models were available in white and are quite rare.

SG JR. : Cherry finish.

SG TV: White finish instead of natural/"limed mahogany". Discontinued after 1964, although some subsequent SG Jr. models had a white finish.

SG SPECIAL: A cherry finish was standard, and a white finish was also available.

Occasionally the white finish in the original SG series from the Sixties is referred to as a "TV" finish as well, but that's technically not quite correct since white was a finish option on the SG Standard and SG Special, as well as on the SG Jr. once the SG TV was discontinued.

Another option on all original SGs was a vibrato arm. On the earliest Customs and Standards these were an unusual sideways type that proved to be a bit too complicated; they were later replaced by a simpler, more traditional style with a flexible plate.

SGs underwent structural and cosmetic changes in the mid-Sixties including different vibrato styles and pickguards that extended to both sides of the instruments' faces.

The advent of the Seventies saw the SG line experience major changes. The SG CUSTOM was the only style that retained its name, but it was severely overhauled. The only finish it became available in was Walnut; it still had three pickups and block fret markers beginning on the first fret. However, the pickguard was an elevated triangular type (unlike all previous SG scratchplates, which had been flush-mounted), and the controls were housed in a plate that was semi-circular.

SG DELUXE: Replaced the SG Standard, and was similar to its predecessor except for **smaller block fret markers beginning on the first fret**, and a pickguard and control layout that matched the new SG Custom.

SG PROFESSIONAL: Replaced the SG Special, and was also similar to its predecessor, except for the new pickguard and control layout.

The single pickup SG Jr. was discontinued in 1971, and as an alternative to it and the Melody Maker line (which had also been discontinued), Gibson introduced the SG 100, SG 200 and SG 250 budget guitars in 1971, along with the SB series of budget bass guitars. These were soon replaced by the SG I, SG II and SG III, along with associated basses. Please see this chapter's section on promotional Gibsons for details.

The 1971 mainline SGs and associated promotional SGs are the least desirable of any SG series. The Custom, Deluxe and Professional all had Gibson/Bigsby vibrato options.

In late 1972, however, some changes began taking shape, not the least of which was a return to the "Custom-Standard-Special" naming system. New alternatives included larger, rectangular tune-a-matic bridges by Schaller, and the SG Special got mini-humbucking pickups with polepieces. Flush-mount pickguards also returned.

In 1973, SG Customs and Standards began to look more like their Sixties predecessors, although the Standard maintained its smaller block fret markers, and both models kept the larger bridges.

As the SG entered the Eighties, Gibson introduced other promotional SGs such as the SG Firebrand and the "SG" (see promotional section). Other modifications in the early part of the decade included the SG Standard receiving an overhaul which included a new bridge.

Throughout this decade, Gibson introduced several SG variants (including re-issues, beginning with the 1986 "SG '62"), and as they are all relatively current models we will not spend too much time on them here.

Some SGs were called SG Deluxe and were available in several finishes. The Gibson Special was an SG variant that had been born in Kalamazoo but its production was switched to Nashville.

Various SGs introduced in the Eighties included the SG Special 400 (three pickups), SG Elite, SG '90 Double, and SG '90 Single.

Now in production in various types for nearly three decades as of this writing, the SG remains one of the most often seen Gibson guitars in music.

The other major Gibson model from the Sixties was the Firebird series, which was much less popular than the SG series. First appearing in 1963, a Firebird at first glance appeared to be a melted Explorer; i.e, they were odd-shaped but were more contoured than the Fifties modernistic guitar. Closer inspection revealed, however, that they were the first Gibson solidbodies to feature "neck-through" construction. Their sculpted pegheads featured rear-projecting, "banjo"-type tuners, and their pickups were mini-humbuckers with no polepieces.

The original 1963 series of Firebirds was as follows:

FIREBIRD I: Single pickup, combination bridge/tailpiece, dot fret markers.

FIREBIRD III: Two pickups, separate bridge and vibrato tailpiece, dot fret markers.

FIREBIRD V: Two pickups, separate bridge and fancier vibrato tailpiece, "trapezoid" fret markers beginning on third fret.

FIREBIRD VII: The ultimate original Firebird had three pickups, separate bridge with fancier vibrato tailpiece, and block fret markers beginning on the first fret. It was also the only guitar in the original series to have gold-plated hardware and an ebony fretboard.

All Firebirds came in standard sunburst finish but were also available in custom colors. They also all featured a red Firebird logo on their white pickguards. Apparently there was a connection between the features on each Firebird and the "Jr.-Special-Standard-Custom" designations as applied to other Gibson solidbodies.

After 1965 (and following a change in Gibson's management), Gibson Firebirds took on the appearance of a more conventional solidbody guitar, and looked suspiciously like Fenders. Some wags have stated that the Firebird was "flipped over" for all intents and purposes, and the first series of Firebirds has generally been referred to as the "reverse" series, while the second series has been dubbed "non-reverse". Banjo-type tuners were replaced by conventional tuners, and pickup toggle switches were replaced by slider-type switches.. Although the model numbers remained the same (as did standard sunburst finishes with custom color options) the guitars themselves were different:

FIREBIRD I: Two P-90 pickups, separate bridge with vibrato tailpiece, dot neck markers.

FIREBIRD III: Three P-90 pickups, otherwise similar to non-reverse Firebird I.

FIREBIRD V: Two mini-humbuckers, separate bridge with fancier vibrato tailpiece, dot neck markers.

FIREBIRD VII: Three mini-humbuckers, and gold parts; otherwise similar to non-reverse Firebird V.

All non-reverse Firebirds had set-in/glued-on neck construction instead of neck-through construction. What's more, all non-reverse Firebirds were routed for three pickups; even if two were used instead of three the extra space was hidden under the scratchplate.

Some "transitional" Firebirds (combining features from both series) do exist, and Gibson has occasionally reissued Firebirds; generally the re-issues conform to the style of the original "reverse" series. Such was the case with the Bicentennial Firebird, which featured a red and blue logo.

A rare and odd Firebird known as the Firebird II appeared in 1982. It had many features previously unseen on any other style of Firebird, including full-size humbuckers and active circuitry. Its body style looked suspiciously like a modified RD body; it was yet another attempt by Gibson to use up their "Artist" active circuitry boards, as the company had issued "Les Paul Artist" and "ES Artist" models in 1979. Firebird IIs had mahogany bodies with bound maple tops (another Firebird first) in assorted finishes.

Other Sixties Gibsons that will receive attention elsewhere include promotional instruments such as Melody Makers, as well as basses.

THE SEVENTIES:
L5S, L6S, BOLT-ONS, ETC.

This decade didn't see any new innovation from Gibson in their solidbody lineup until 1973, when they introduced the L5S, which at the time of its premier was their highest-priced production solidbody. The L5S was a single-cutaway guitar that was a bit different from a single-cutaway Les Paul; its body was thinner and featured very wide binding. It came in cherry sunburst or a natural finish, and featured gold hardware, including a tailpiece like the L-5 archtop. The first L5Ss had large, oval-shaped low impedance pickups like the Les Paul Recording model; in late 1974 regular humbuckers replaced the low impedance pickups. This model was quite exquisite but commercially unsuccessful.

L6S: The underrated L6S was introduced in 1974. It too had a single-cutaway body, albeit a different style from either Les Pauls or L5Ss. (I once heard someone comment that the L6S looked like a Les Paul that had been run over by a steamroller.) It was the first Gibson to feature a 24-fret neck, and it also had new, powerful "Super Humbucking" pickups. Despite the innovations involved with this model, it too was a dud sales-wise.

Bolt-on Gibsons from the Seventies included the Marauder and the S-1; both also had arrowhead-shaped headstocks. Likewise there were basses with bolt-on necks, which will be discussed in the section on basses.

The much-maligned RD series came out in 1977, and apparently went nowhere fast. Consisting of three guitars and two basses, the RDs looked like melted Firebirds to most musicians (and as previously stated, Firebirds looked like melted Explorers!). The fanciest of the three guitars and the fancier of the two basses had active circuitry; they were known as the "RD Artist". The mid-grade guitar, the "RD Custom" offered less complex active circuitry, and the "Standard" guitar and bass were passive instruments. This series was so unsuccessful that Gibson had to release other styles of instruments with active electronics to use up the circuit boards.

So it appears that Gibson's Les Pauls and SGs were still the mainline instruments for the company through the Seventies, while almost any innovation Gibson attempted in the solidbody field ultimately ended up as a commercial failure.

Before the Seventies are left behind, it seem appropriate to diverge from the solidbody saga to note two styles of Les Pauls that surfaced in the Seventies **that were not solidbody instruments**. The Les Paul Jumbo showed up around 1970 for a short time; it was a flat-top acoustic with a single, low impedance pickup between the soundhole and neck. The Les Paul Signature was a semi-solid instrument that used an ES-335 body as a foundation; there was also a matching Les Paul Signature bass. Signatures weren't around too long, either.

THE EIGHTIES:
MORE SLUGS and BACK TO THE FUTURE

Throughout the Eighties, Gibson once again apparently counted on its mainline instruments, while other attempts at new instruments didn't seem to work. Examples of Gibsons that didn't catch on included other bolt-on series, with such models as the Victory, Challenger, Corvus (which had a body that looked like a can opener), Invader, and A-300 (which had three P-90 pickups and was made from leftover Victory bodies). An upgrade Corvus variant, the Futura, had a set-in neck, but still looked like a can opener...

Some late Eighties guitars looked dangerously close to a Fender Stratocaster if one examined their silhouettes; such models included the US-1 and the U-2. Other Gibson solidbodies came and went during the decade as well, including the Spirit and ES-335S.

About the major upgrade style of Gibson that has yet to be addressed is the double-neck type; these have been made on a limited basis since 1959.

So now that we've examined the wide variety of Gibson's solidbody electrics by decade, it's time to step back (and down) a bit and take a look at their promotional instruments, again on a decade-by-decade basis:

Technically, about the only promotional Gibson from the Fifties would have been the Les Paul Jr., although the Melody Maker was introduced in 1959. Originally a thin, single-cutaway instrument with one or two small, single coil pickups, the Melody Maker soon evolved to a symmetrical, double cutaway style in 1961. This shape was modified somewhat in 1964, and in 1966 the pointed double-cutaway SG body was placed on the Melody Maker; the SG style remained on the Melody Maker until it was discontinued in 1970. All Melody Makers, regardless of body shape, had smaller headstocks than those found on other Gibson instruments. Some SG-type Melody Makers had three pickups and/or vibratos, and Melody Maker 12-string guitars and basses were also made.

As noted in the previous paragraph, the Melody Maker line carried Gibson through the Sixties in the budget-priced market, but they also made the bolt-on Kalamazoo line in that decade.

Around 1971, three SG-type guitars replaced the Melody Maker line (as well as the SG Jr.); they were the SG 100, SG 200 and SG 250. Like the newly re-styled mainline SGs of the same time period, they had elevated triangular pickguards, and their controls were housed in an oval-shaped metal plate. This promotional series kept the small oval-shaped pickups like those found on Melody Makers. The SG 100 had one pickup installed at an angle near the neck, the SG 200 had two pickups and the SG 250 was exactly like the SG 200 except for a cherry sunburst finish (the SG 100 and 200 came in walnut or cherry finishes). For what it's worth, this series had headstocks that matched the body color instead of the normal black headstock (apparently this was the first Gibson series to have such). Also of note around this time was the semi-solid ES-320, rarest of all Gibson thinline semi-solids. It also had two Melody Maker type pickups, controls in an oval metal plate, and most of these also had matching headstocks. Although much rarer than its SG-shaped cousins, it was technically a beginner's thinline and is not particularly valuable.

The bodies of this series were somewhat oversized, and in late 1972 they were replaced (respectively) by the SG I, SG II and SG III. These were roughly the same instruments except they used mini-humbuckers with no polepieces, and the SG I's solitary pickup was located near the bridge instead of the neck.

Around 1978, Gibson introduced an odd, single cutaway instrument known as "The Paul". It resembled a Les Paul, but came in a plain, natural finish with open coil humbuckers (no covers), no pickguard and a matching headstock. It was apparently intended as a no-frills Les Paul, and inspired other promotional instruments in the early Eighties.

The early Eighties saw other "no-frills" Gibson instruments introduced to attempt to appeal to the budget market. "The SG" was, as might be expected, an SG-shaped associate of "The Paul". Other natural-finished guitars popped up later under the "Firebrand" series banner. These were similar to The Paul and The SG, and came in three body styles: LP Firebrand (Les Paul shape), SG Firebrand (SG shape) and ES Firebrand (ES-335S shape). The Gibson logo was embossed into the Firebrands' headstocks and were not colored black or gold like other Gibson logos.

A step-up series was the Firebrand Deluxe, which came in stock finishes with a normal black headstock and gold Gibson logo.

Obviously, many musicians considered the Eighties bolt-ons such as the Invader and Corvus to have been promotional instruments as well, but Gibson seems to have gradually phased out of seeking the budget segment of the guitar market, preferring to sell its imported Epiphone by Gibson instruments to beginners, casual players, etc.

BASS GUITARS

As previously noted, Gibson's first Electric Bass was introduced in 1953, but it differed from the ground-breaking Fender bass in two ways; the violin-shaped Gibson Electric Bass had a short scale of 30 1/2" and a glued on neck, whereas the Fender bass had a full-size 34" scale and a bolt-on neck. The Gibson bass also had rear-projecting, banjo-type tuners. It became known as the EB-1 when a second bass, the EB-2, was introduced around 1958, and was soon discontinued in favor of the EB-0.

EB-2: A semi-solid cousin of the ES-335 thinline series. Unlike the EB-1, it was eventually available in a two-pickup version (EB-2D).

EB-0: The first version of this single pickup replacement had the offset, double-cutaway body shape of Les Paul Jrs. and Specials from the same time period, as well as banjo-type tuners. Eventually, it assumed the classic SG shape (circa 1961) with perpendicular tuners.

EB-6: Gibson's "baritone guitar" originally had a semi-solid thinline configuration when introduced in 1960, but it too was given an SG-style body, this time in 1962; however, one source indicates that it was also **discontinued** in 1962!

EB-3: This was Gibson's workhorse bass for years; it was basically a two-pickup version of the EB-0 and came in the SG shape only. It was also available in a long-scale version for a couple of years (EB-3L).

EB-4L: A short-lived model with a single-pickup that had a pickup with "2 + 2" offset polepieces and a three-position tone switch; it too was long scale.

The Seventies also produced some other long scale basses that didn't seem to work for Gibson (as was the case with many guitars introduced in that decade). Among these basses were:

GRABBER: Bolt-on neck, arrowhead headstock, sliding pickup.

G-3: Bolt-on neck; bass equivalent of the S-1 guitar.

RIPPER: Set-in neck, two humbucking pickups, Varitone. The highest-priced of these three basses with the same body style, but none of them really went over.

RD STANDARD AND RD ARTIST: As previously noted, the Standard was a passive bass and the Artist had active electronics. The scale on the RD basses was an unusual 34 1/2" scale. In this writer's opinion, the RD Artist would make a fine studio bass, but as a performance instrument, it would most likely be quite cumbersome.

Like the Seventies, the Eighties saw Gibson make other attempts at the bass market; most of these ventures proved unsuccessful, although like Seventies basses, bass guitars introduced by Gibson in the Eighties were all full-scale instruments.

A bass guitar was available in the early Eighties "Victory" series. It had a bolt-on neck, severe angle cutaways and a humbucking pickup at an equally severe angle. It was somewhat Fender-ish in its appearance.

Throughout the Eighties, Gibson basses based on popular Gibson shapes would turn up, so Flying V basses and Explorer basses will be encountered. They are not particularly that unique except for their body shape.

Basses from the late Eighties included the Gibson IV and Gibson V (these two had arrowhead-shaped headstocks), and the Q-80 and Q-90, which had bodies that were based on Victory basses and four-on-a-side tuners.

Designed with the input of Ned Steinberger, the 20/20 bass looked like a prop from the set of a science fiction movie; it resembled a ray gun, and was available in silver with black hardware. It also had active electronics.

The last series of frontline Gibson basses that needs to be examined (but certainly not the least) is the redoubtable Thunderbird line, which was/is the bass equivalent of the Firebird guitar series. Some might think that anytime a Firebird was issued or reissued, a matching Thunderbird was also released, but that wasn't necessarily the case.

Such **was** the case with original Firebirds and Thunderbirds of 1963; the Thunderbird II had one pickup and the Thunderbird IV had two. Like that era's Firebirds, they featured neck-through construction.

Likewise, the "flipped-over" Firebirds of the mid-Sixties had matching "flipped-over" Thunderbirds as well (same model numbering system). Moreover, there was also a Bicentennial Thunderbird, also with a red and blue logo.

Some Firebird re-issues other than the Bicentennial series did not have corresponding Thunderbirds, however, and it is not believed that an active electronics "Thunderbird II" was issued when the "Firebird II" was made in 1982. The situation has also been the reverse at times; the 1988 Gibson catalog showed a Thunderbird bass but no Firebird! It was a neck-through "reverse" style with black hardware and a "three-point" bridge/tailpiece like those found on the RD basses.

Most budget basses by Gibson were from the early Seventies; they were the bass equivalents of early Seventies sub-series guitars, and are as equally scorned as their six-string counterparts. Models included the SB 100, SB 200, SB 300, SB 400, SB 350 and SB 450.

It now appears that Gibson is not pursuing the bass segment of the market as actively as they may have in the past. Most of their innovations of the last couple of decades in bass guitars have not particularly been successful but some of their interesting basses such as the Thunderbird will still apparently move well whenever they are made. Otherwise, the imported Epiphone by Gibson line appears to be the company's main bass venture as of this writing.

Obviously, this chapter on Gibson has been much longer than the Fender chapter, but the line has always been much more varied, and of course, there are positive and negative aspects to such a marketing strategy. Gibson has a fine, proud tradition, and is still seeking to be a factor in the American fretted instrument market as their Centennial year approaches. Their re-issues and limited editions still command immediate attention from musicians, and many of the current versions of some of their "old favorites" are still selling well.

DEFINITIONS:
"SUB-BRANDS", "HOUSE BRANDS", and INSTRUMENTS
"MADE OVERSEAS UNDER NAME LICENSING"

Much of the apparent confusion among persons with a beginning or casual interest in instruments with American brand names involves situations where a guitar or bass might be cited as having one or more of the preceding terms applied to it. Most often, someone thinks that he/she has something that is worth much more than it actually is, so this chapter will concentrate on attempting to alert the reader to the fact that in many cases certain brands and models might be less valuable than their owners might claim.

SUB-BRANDS
The prefix "sub" means "under", so all of the "sub-brands" cited in the chapter that lists American guitar brand names would have been (or are) lower-priced than another brand (or brands) made by the same manufacturer. Examples include:

MANUFACTURER	"FLAGSHIP" BRAND	SUB-BRAND (S)
Gibson	Gibson	Epiphone, Kalamazoo
Valco	National	Supro
Harmony	Harmony	Stella
Kay	Kay	Kamico
Gretsch	Gretsch	Rex (early 1900s)

Adding to the confusion these days is the fact that most instrument manufacturers would probably be selling sub-brands (or even lower-priced instruments with their "flagship" brand name) that are made overseas; an example of this trend was Gibson's decision around 1970 to apply the Epiphone brand name to an imported line which was distributed by Gibson. The preceding list involved domestic instruments only.

The general trend of a sub-brand being worth less than a flagship brand also holds true in the used/vintage market as well. Most sub-brands were made to hit a lower pricing point and get a segment of the retail market that a high-grade manufacturer might otherwise miss. Such manufacturers chose to offer a different brand name rather than place their own name on a lower-priced/promotional instrument series.

Some sub-brands may have started up in the U.S., but after a brief time were shifted overseas by the manufacturer. Fender's "Bullet" series was a promotional **domestic** line for a short time, but soon went off-shore. On the flip side, their "Squier" series is reportedly going to have some models that are domestic rather than imported, so it gets confusing. Current "Bullet" and "Squier" series should have "by Fender" and the country of origin on their headstocks.

However, some manufacturers have occasionally produced a higher-priced, fancier series of instruments, and have placed an alternate brand name on such instruments' headstocks (Ovation has a high-end line called Adamas, for example). For lack of a better term, such series might be referred to as "super-brands", but very few examples exist. Once again, there might be an import factor even with such super-brands.

HOUSE BRANDS
Over two dozen of the brands cited in the chapter on American brand names were designated as "house brands". House brands are names given by a specific retailer or distributor to a line of instruments that they will sell. The most popular example, of course, is Sears "Silvertone" instruments, and in some cases, some companies may have sold more than one brand name (Montgomery Ward brands included Airline and Sherwood).

Most domestic-made house brand instruments began disappearing in the late Sixties, as many retailers began switching to foreign-made guitars and basses. Accordingly, most of the Chicago-area manufacturers began going out of business during the same time period.

Of course, the vast majority of domestically-made house instruments were promotionally-priced, and were made by companies that tended to specialize in budget instruments. Accordingly, most house brand guitars or basses fetch about the same amounts as their manufacturers' own brand name counterparts; in either case, the amounts aren't too much, but there may be some exceptions.

Some rare or perhaps even unknown house brands may be encountered from time to time; as the manufacturer is most likely extinct, there may not be any records to determine what retailer or distributor marketed the brand name. Such a "dead end" may or may not increase the value of a house brand instrument, but in some cases, attempting to determine who sold the brand name can make for some interesting research.

NAME LICENSING

Name licensing given to overseas factories by a U.S. guitar company (**which may or may not still be making instruments domestically**) puts an originally American brand name on an imported guitar. This situation is exactly like business decisions made by the U.S. automobile industry and other American companies; labor is less expensive off-shore. As is the case with Washburn, the brand name found on some foreign instruments may have been American at one time, but the U.S. manufacturer has been out of business for **decades!**

Here's an alphabetized list of American brand names that are either being made **domestically and overseas, or overseas only if the American manufacturer has gone out of business:**

CHARVEL: Originally, Wayne Charvel has an association with Jackson, and he subsequently designed a series of instruments for Gibson (this association was short-lived). It appears that all Charvel instruments are now imports, and should have "Made in Japan" on them. There's now even a "sub-brand" from the same company called Charvette.

DEAN: Originally, domestic Deans are unusual-shaped, solid-body instruments that are distinguished by their oversized, "V"-shaped headstock. Dean began importing instruments as well, and these imported instruments have a different headstock (and they do not have the country of origin on them!). The imports' headstocks are somewhat tapered or "arrow"-shaped, except that there is a small notch where the "point" would be. Dean instruments with "six-on-a-side" or "four-on-a-side" tuners should also be imports.

EPIPHONE: As explained in the chapter on American brands of guitars, Epiphone has been made both domestically and overseas, and was also a domestically-made Gibson sub-brand for about ten years. It's been a foreign-made sub-brand since 1970, and any guitar that has "Epiphone by Gibson" on it should be an import; i.e., when Epiphone was a domestic sub-brand, only its own name was found on the headstock (as is still the case with some imports). Confused? It gets a bit more complex: Every once in a while the author has encountered a post-1970 Epiphone that was made in the U.S.! For instance, a 1982 "Epiphone Spirit" was spotted in a music store by yours truly in 1989; it was exactly like a Gibson Spirit of the same time period, and had a Gibson-style serial number and "Made in U.S.A." on the back of the headstock, so it was absolutely legitimate. Gibson owns the rights to the Epiphone name, so they can use it as they please, even if it does get confusing sometimes...

FENDER: Perhaps the most misunderstood brand of all when it comes to name licensing. Fenders can be made domestically or overseas, and as noted earlier in this chapter, the company also markets imported sub-brands. Not only can regular Fender instruments such as Telecasters, Stratocasters and Precision basses come in from overseas with "Made in Japan" on their headstocks, Fender has at times released special "re-issue" instruments, and these faithful reproductions of some of their classic instruments from the Fifties and Sixties may be made domestically or overseas as well. In many re-issue situations, the country where the re-issue was made is not noted on the surface of the instrument. For example, the author was once shown a metallic red Fender Telecaster with the older "spaghetti" logo on its headstock, and its owner proclaimed it to be a 1958 model. It had a very long serial number stamped into its bridge plate, and the serial number began with an "A". Contacting a Fender retailer confirmed that it was a "'62 re-issue" model, made overseas beginning in 1986.

Of course, bona fide old Fenders would not have the country of origin on them either, since at that time they were made only in the U.S. Moreover, an instrument like a real 1958 Tele would not have a long serial number, so if there's any uncertainty as to when what appears to be an old Fender instrument was made, contact a Fender dealer or vintage authority.

At one time, Harmony of Chicago made some acoustic instruments for Fender. While these are relatively rare, like Harmony's own brand of instruments (as well as umpteen house brands made by the Chicago behemoth) Fender guitars made by Harmony are worth very little (especially when compared to a Fender-made acoustic of the same time period!). About the only way to note whether an older Fender acoustic was Fender-made or Harmony-made is the fact that Fender's own instruments would have the classic, six-on-a-side Fender headstock, as well as a classic Fender logo. Harmony-made Fenders would have a three-on-a-side headstock and the Fender name in a solitary color, usually white.

GRETSCH: Once the ultimate brand name in American-made electric guitars, Gretsch has been footballed around a good bit, but any of the old New York-made instruments would be valuable and sought, with the possible exception of certain inexpensive solidbodies such as the Corvette. There were some late Seventies models imported from Mexico (all solidbodies?), and the author saw a solitary ad for a wildly-painted guitar that resembled a Danelectro about the time that the "Traveling Wilburys" album was released in 1988; this instrument was seen in some of the band's videos, and it too was sporting a Gretsch name, despite the fact that it was made in the Far East! Perhaps a bit of stability may have been added in late 1989, when a Japanese manufacturer began making faithful reproductions of the original New York classics. So while the name has apparently been put on instruments produced in as many as four countries, at least the current style of instruments (as of this writing) fits into the "something old, something new" concept. Most of the Gretsch instruments that are found in pawn shops tend to be ones that were "hecho en Mexico", and they are not popular at all.

HARMONY: Brand name has been licensed to overseas manufacturing concerns since the latter Seventies, and like their American namesakes, foreign Harmonys are on the lower end of pricing. The name licensing arrangement apparently even allows "Since 1898" to be placed on the headstocks of foreign Harmonys, so don't let that notation throw you!

KAY: Practically the same status (past and present) as Harmony.

KRAMER: While a relatively new company, Kramer has marketed instruments have been made domestically and overseas. An important thing to remember is that **even imported Kramers will have the company's home office of Neptune, New Jersey noted on a plate on the back of the instrument.** Some imported Kramers will have the country where it was made on a sticker on the back of the headstock, but the sticker is easily removed. "Focus", "Aero-Star" and "Striker" are names of Kramer series that are imported. If in doubt, check with a Kramer dealer.

MARTIN: Martin instruments themselves are made in the U.S., but Martin's "Shenandoah" series is a "hybrid"; most of the components of Shenandoah instruments are made overseas, but the guitars are put through their final assembly stages domestically. The "Sigma" series is imported, as is an electric line known as "Stinger".

NATIONAL: The author has seen some imported instruments and amplifiers with a National brand name, so apparently the name is/was licensed for overseas production like so many other American brands that are no longer being made in the U.S.

REGAL: Import only; Regal went out of business domestically in 1954, but the name rights were sold to Harmony, which **was** still producing domestic instruments then.

RICH, B.C.: Another relatively new company that has marketed domestic and imported instruments; many imported B.C. Rich instruments will have "N.J. Series" on the headstock, but that's not always the case. Contact a dealer or the manufacturer for authentication.

SCHECTER: Upgrade utilitarian line made both domestically and overseas.

STELLA: This former Harmony sub-brand is being made overseas only, as is the case with Harmony itself.

VEGA: Formerly domestic; imported since the early Eighties; name rights sold back to an American Company in 1989.

WASHBURN: Out of business in the U.S. since 1930; Washburn is apparently one of the most successful import lines, marketing electrics and acoustics.

To sum up, perhaps it might help clear up some questions about certain brand names if the names of some of the **foreign manufacturers** of instruments were listed, as well as the **brands** that they make. Admittedly, this is somewhat of an overseas version of what Kay and Harmony were doing some decades ago; some of the brand names made overseas are of course original names (Yamaha, for example), some are former U.S. brand names that are now being made exclusively overseas (Washburn), and some may be being made both in the U.S. and overseas (Fender). Yet other brands found here may have American-sounding names, but have always been made overseas (Bill Lawrence).

The following list was published in the October 1990 issue of <u>Music Trades</u> magazine, and is concerned exclusively with Far East manufacturers, since they comprise the vast majority of imported instruments marketed in the U.S. Following the designation of each country, manufacturers will be listed alphabetically, and following each manufacturer, the **brands** that each manufacturer makes will be listed (also in alphabetical order):

JAPAN:
ATLANSIA: Atlansia
CHU SIN GAKKI: Charvel
ESP: ESP, Focus, Kramer
FUJIGEN GAKKI: Casio, Fender, Greco, Ibanez, Heartfield, Squire, Westone
HEADWAY: Riverhead
KASUGA: Blade, Tune, Washburn, Yamaha
KAWAI: Fernandes, Kawai, Rockoon
MORRIS: Aircraft, Fender, Hurricane, Bill Lawrence, Morris
SHIMOKURA: Boss Axe, Chandler, Mosrite
TAKAMINE: Takamine
TERADA: Aria, Epiphone, Terada
TOKAI: Aria, Greco, Tokai
YAMAHA: Yamaha

KOREA:
CORT: Cort, Hohner, Kramer
SAEHAN: Applause, B.C. Rich, Celebrity, Fernandes, Ovation, Vester, Westone
SAMICK: Aria, Epiphone, Hondo, Marathon, Samick, Vantage, Washburn
YOUNG CHANG: Fender, Fenix, Hurricane, Morris, Squier

TAIWAN:
YAMAHA: Yamaha

Notice that some of the brands with what appear to have been originally Japanese brand names are now being made in other countries as well.

To complicate things even further, the author heard a rumor in mid-1990 that some instruments were going to soon be made in India and exported to the U.S ; said instruments were going to be marketed by Fender, most likely under the Squier sub-brand name. Ultimately, some Indian-made Strats have been encoutered.

As of this writing, it appears that there is an increasing trend by some Japanese companies to increase their manufacturing capabilities in other countries; many economists consider the Japanese economy to be hyper-inflated, and examples of higher-priced Japanese-made instruments include some Ibanez and ESP guitars that list for around $1500, which puts them in direct competition with many fine American-made instruments.

So not only are foreign companies making many brand names, just as Kay and Harmony did in their time, some companies are letting the brand name be manufactured in countries other than the original! In a way, it's interesting to compare what may be occurring in Japan these days with the history of the American guitar-making industry some decades ago.

So while sub-brands, house brands and instruments made overseas under name licensing are generally not too valuable, it's important to remember that there may be some fine instruments in the mix, such as the current Fender and Gretsch imported re-issues. As these styles are relatively new, time will tell how desirable such high-end imports will ultimately become.

Hopefully, this chapter has cleared up at least some of the mysteries surrounding certain instruments.

TERMS AND CONDITIONS

No, this isn't a chapter about contracts! Instead, the terminology involved with guitars when it comes to selling and/or collecting will be examined, including some descriptive phrases that specific major manufacturers apply to some of their own brands. We'll also take a look at how most guitar enthusiasts and vintage authorities would classify a certain instrument as being in a specific "condition", depending on how much "wear and tear" is found on said instrument.

"VINTAGE" VS. "USED"

First and foremost, it seems appropriate to discuss the term **"VINTAGE"**. In most states, owners of automobiles may apply for an "antique vehicle" license plate if their car is 20-25 years old, and along this line of thinking, most guitar enthusiasts seem to use the quarter-century mark as a guideline to differentiate between "vintage" and simply "used". This terminology is usually applied **regardless** of the value, rarity or desirability of the instrument, so from a retailing standpoint a fancy Gibson guitar and a promotional Silvertone instrument that were both made in the Fifties would both be considered as "vintage" guitars.

"RARE", "DISCONTINUED", and "COLLECTOR'S ITEM"

There is often much confusion and overlap in retail situations when the following terms are used or heard if guitars are being discussed: **"RARE"**, **"DISCONTINUED"** and the much-abused **"COLLECTOR'S ITEM"**. Please note that a guitar (whether "vintage" or "used") can have any of these three terms applied to it in any combination!

If a guitar is **"RARE"**, it of course was made in small quantities, and naturally the extreme limit of rarity is the one-of-a-kind, custom-made instrument.

"DISCONTINUED" instruments may or may not be "rare", and whether or not they will ultimately become sought-after cannot be predicted. If a guitar happens to be an older brand name and American-made, the fact that it might be a discontinued model is a "plus" in a retail situation, but sometimes "discontinued" is the only "plus" that certain vintage guitars will have!

The term **"COLLECTOR'S ITEM"** is mis-used so often, I usually cringe if and when I hear someone pronounce an instrument to be collectible, regardless of whether I'm in a pawn shop, flea market, music store or private residence. Usually, such an individual who states that a particular guitar is a "collector's item" thinks it is such simply because it might happen to be "rare" and/or "discontinued", and the individual also usually doesn't have any documentation to back up such a pronouncement.

Whether or not a guitar is "collectible" depends largely upon its "desirability", and the vintage guitar market is subject to an enormous amount of volatility. In the mid-to-late Eighties, the term "Strat-mania" was heard throughout the vintage market; Fender Stratocaster guitars from the Fifties and Sixties skyrocketed in demand (and price, of course), but as the decade ended their desirability (therefore, their value) had dropped off considerably.

As stated in the introduction, such volatility in the vintage market is one of several reasons why many guitar enthusiasts don't like to see instrument prices in a "fixed" situation, and instrument appraisals from better dealers should have **"current market value"** beside the price and should be **dated** as well.

Having differentiated in the terms "rare", "discontinued" and "collector's item", it now seems appropriate to list several guitars as token examples of where each term could be applied (including combinations of terms), and why:

RARE: A particular model is rare whose known production totals are small. Example - in the year 1921 C. F. Martin made one (1) 000-28K koa wood auditorium sized guitar and that was the only one ever made. Any custom-made instrument with specifications ordered by a particular player to suit his/her own needs. As previously noted, many companies such as Alembic, Pensa-Suhr and others tend to specialize in instruments with custom features, and the higher pricing structure reflects this strategy.

DISCONTINUED: Some series, such as Fender's Telecaster Thin-lines, have ultimately become sought after, while Fender's Coronado thin-line f-hole series (made around the same time) never has been much in demand.

COLLECTOR'S ITEM: As previously stated, subject to change. Of course, some guitars such as late Fifties Gibson Les Paul Standard guitars (in sunburst finishes) will always be sought.

RARE AND DISCONTINUED: Some oddball house brands made by any of several Chicago-area manufacturers. Such instruments are similar to many others (including the manufacturer's own brand name) with the exception of the name on the headstock (House brands are examined in detail in the preceding chapter).

RARE AND COLLECTIBLE: Gibson's ultra-high Citation arch-top acoustic electric. Still being made on a special-order basis, which may mean that each Citation may have custom features ordered by its owner.

DISCONTINUED AND COLLECTIBLE: Ampeg/Dan Armstrong Plexiglass guitars and basses from the late Sixties and early Seventies. A good many of these were made, and while not particularly fantastic utility instruments, the fact remains that their clear bodies made them among the most cosmetically cool guitars and basses ever produced.

RARE, DISCONTINUED AND COLLECTIBLE: Original 1958 Gibson Explorers and Flying Vs.

"UTILITY" VS. "COLLECTIBLE" VS. "INVESTMENT" INSTRUMENTS

"Valuable" and "Desirable" (and derivative words) are terms that may be heard often, but like "Collector's Item", they tend to be unreliable and abused; that's because of the aforementioned volatility in the vintage market and other factors. While clean examples of classic American guitars will always have a relatively healthy value to them, the rise and decline of Stratocaster prices as noted earlier is exemplary of how the vintage market is capable of behaving like a roller coaster.

As for the term "desirable", the important thing to consider is whether an instrument is desirable to a particular customer as either a **UTILITY PIECE** (to be played, either professionally or for enjoyment), a **COLLECTOR'S INSTRUMENT,** or as an instrument to be used as an **INVESTMENT** (to be turned by the customer at a later date).

I feel that any single instrument's desirability ultimately rests within the **eye (and wallet) of the customer.** I am not a vintage instrument retailer, which is the reason I do not appraise instruments for stores or individuals. I **do** have a modest collection, and in some cases I will buy an instrument in the hopes of selling it or trading it some time down the road, in an effort to improve my own collection (which any collector would normally do). So in other words, one person may be considering an instrument or instruments for any one of the three reasons cited in the previous paragraph, and the reason may vary with the individual guitar! I play, I have a collection and I will sometimes buy to sell or trade later.

"STAR POWER"

Another term that is not often heard but that figures into the desirability of some instruments is "star power", and in the opinion of many guitar enthusiasts, including yours truly, it is perhaps the most misunderstood and abused "concept" of all. Many players who are just beginning to learn about guitars seek to own a particular brand and model simply because their favorite guitar hero plays one. While this is generally an unfortunate line of thinking, it nevertheless figures into retail sales of instruments, and a selected list of guitars and noted musicians who have played that particular model will be found in the chapter entitles "As Played By..."

Of course, sometimes the idea of "star power" can figure into vintage instrument collecting as well. In the spring of 1990, the noted auction house of Sotheby's sold the Fender Stratocaster that was played by Jimi Hendrix at Woodstock in 1969. It was purchased by an Italian buyer for the sum of approximately **$320,000!!!** One vintage authority who heard about the price was incredulous, stating that the value of the instrument was only about $1,000 and that the buyer must have "a poor ratio of money to brains". The vintage authority also wondered what the price of the instrument would have been if Hendrix had played a cheap Harmony-made instrument at Woodstock, and envisioned an even more bizarre scenario, stating that an Elvis Presley fan would pay the same amount for a guitar that had been played by the King, regardless of whether the guitar was a classic C.F. Martin D-28 or a cheap Sears Silvertone.

LIMITED EDITIONS and RE-ISSUES

So much for basic terms concerning instruments, what about a so-called "**LIMITED EDITION**"? First of all, for any instrument to be considered as such, it should have some type of authentication such as a certificate of registration ("This is #_____ of a total of _____ made") and/or some kind of plaque or medallion built onto the guitar itself. Just because an owner proclaims an instrument to be a limited edition doesn't make it one. In many cases, books or guitar manufacturers will be able to verify that a specific instrument is or is not a limited edition, just as the same sources could help in authenticating normal production instruments.

A definitive example of a limited edition guitar is Fender's 1979 "Silver Anniversary" Stratocaster. Each one had a certificate of registration, and each also had a small plate on the back (where the neck bolts into the body) with a special six digit serial number, the first two digits of which were "25" (to note the twenty fifth year of production); the years 1954-1979 were also stamped onto this plate. Approximately 10,000 Silver Anniversary Stratocasters were made (which would of course use up all of the possible numbers for the remaining four digits of the six-digit serial number); while that may seem like a fairly large amount to be a so-called "limited edition", keep in mind that one music magazine estimated that in the late Eighties there were **eighteen million** guitarists in the United States.

Some manufacturers have their own systems for designating certain guitars as limited production runs in addition to the aforementioned certificates and medallions/plaques. Some examples include:

(1) GIBSON GUITARS WITH A "CUSTOM SHOP" DECAL ON THE BACK OF THE HEADSTOCK: "Custom Shop Original" may mean that the instrument was made in Gibson's Custom Shop, or that the item may simply have a single unique feature, such as a custom color. Usually "Custom Shop Originals" are limited to one or two instruments. However, "Custom Shop Edition" Gibsons most likely will have been made in a special production run instead of in the Custom Shop, and Custom Shop Editions will have special cosmetic and/or electronic features. It is suspected that some Custom Shop Editions are made to use up some extra parts that might otherwise go unused by Gibson.

(2) GIBSON GUITARS WITH "SHOWCASE EDITION" OR "LIMITED COLORS EDITION" ON BACK OF HEADSTOCK: In the late Eighties, Gibson began a somewhat controversial practice of releasing a "Showcase Edition" each month; each edition was limited to 200 pieces. They were simply production instruments with slight alterations, such as black hardware or an extra pickup. Later, "Limited Colors Edition" came along, which were stock instruments in unusual colors, also limited to 200 per month (the color changed each month).

(3) FENDER GUITARS WITH HEADSTOCK SERIAL NUMBERS BEGINNING WITH A "C": Indicates that the guitar is part of Fender's "Collector's Series" that was made in the early Eighties.

These three examples show how a guitar may be letting someone know that it's a bit unique, even if there's no documentation to go with it.

For all of the hoopla generated by the marketing of "limited edition" guitars (and other guitars with similar designations), some guitar enthusiasts feel that this sales ploy is inappropriate for two reasons:

(1) There seems to be at least a subliminal suggestion on the part of the manufacturer that just because a guitar is made in small quantities, such a guitar will ultimately become collectible and will appreciate in value. **That ain't necessarily so,** unless these manufacturers have got a crystal ball and can predict the future of the guitar market.

(2) A purchaser of such a guitar might feel the instrument should be stored instead of played, in order to keep it in absolutely pristine condition. If that's the case, it seems sort of sad that the instrument will simply be looked at occasionally rather than be used for the reason it was made, to play music.

Some people tend to confuse a "Limited Edition" instrument with a "**RE-ISSUE**" instrument. The two terms are not synonymous, and "**re-issues**" **may or may not be** "**limited editions**".

Whenever a major company announces a "re-issue", the instrument in question is based on a popular style from some time ago. However, in some cases the "re-issue" is not an exact reproduction of the original (Gibson has been cited by some for this practice of not remaining precisely faithful to the "Real McCoy").

Some re-issues may be limited editions, such as the 1976 Gibson Bicentennial Firebird. It was supposed to be a short-lived instrument, but records indicate that Bicentennial Firebirds were made into 1978, and that the total number of Firebirds made for the Bicentennial was greater than any other edition of that body style up to that point in time. Technically, the 1976 Firebird was an early Sixties "reverse" Firebird III re-issue, but it differed from the original in that it had gold hardware and a different bridge/tailpiece design.

On the flip side of the same coin, Gibson's Firebird re-issue of 1990 matched the specifications of the 1976 Firebird except for chrome hardware and "trapezoid"-shaped fret markers beginning on the third fret. **The 1990 Firebird re-issue has not been designated as a limited edition** so it is assumed that it will stay in production as long as the market demand will support it.

Fender makes many re-issue instruments that are **very close to the original instrument.** These are referred to as Vintage Re-Issues and may be made domestically or overseas. Some of them may be limited editions as well; usually the limited edition will be designated as such due to its color.

Rickenbacker is another manufacturer that has had considerable success with its Vintage Series, which includes not only reproductions of classic early "Rick" guitars, but a bass guitar and a 3/4 scale guitar re-issue as well. The letter "V" appearing in the middle of a Rickenbacker instrument's model number indicates that it is part of their Vintage Series.

So simply because something is designated as "rare", "discontinued", a "collector's item", a "limited edition" (or similar terms) or any other descriptive phrase, "value" and "desirability" can depend entirely on the individual circumstances and instruments. "Rare", "discontinued" and "limited edition" are terms that can be sometimes documented, and if that's the case with a particular instrument, such terms should be used when selling it. "Collector's item", however, is a bit more nebulous, and such pronouncements by owners should be taken with a grain of salt until investigated.

CONDITIONS OF USED INSTRUMENTS

Another factor that of course affects an instrument's "value" and/or "desirability" deserves to be considered separately, and that is the CONDITION that an instrument is in when it is pawned or sold. Even a guitar that is rare, discontinued, a collector's item **and** a limited edition can be completely worthless if it is in atrocious condition (re: the 1976 Gibson Bicentennial Firebird cited in the introduction to this book). Obviously, a clean instrument of any brand or model will fetch more than a similar one that is in terrible shape. Many collectors would rather have a mint condition Sears guitar (most likely for trade) than a Gibson that's ruined.

Here is a checklist of guitar parts that need to be examined whenever a transaction involving an instrument is being considered (retail sale, private sale, pawn shop loan, etc.). The more problems with these parts an instrument has, the less desirable (therefore the less valuable) it will be:

1.   Signs of damage, including cracks (especially behind the nut and at the heel of the neck), neck pulling away from body at heel, or signs of owner abuse.
2.   Non-working truss rod. A frozen or broken truss rod, or one which simply isn't effective in removing a forward or backbow, is usually an unmistakable signal that you should walk away from the instrument.
3.   Worn finish (body and/or neck)
4.   Worn and/or warped pickguard
5.   Corroded hardware
6.   Missing original parts (including knobs, etc.)
7.   Warped/bowed neck (sight it down the length; many instruments have necks so bowed, a player could slice hard-boiled eggs with the strings)
8.   Worn frets (move each string aside on the fretboard near the nut and see if frets in that area have any small grooves worn in them)
9.   Yellowed areas such as binding (this is caused by cigarette smoke, and some guitar bodies that may have originally been white or natural may have turned an almost butterscotch-color due to their having been played in numerous honky-tonks). However, some guitar buffs consider slightly yellowed binding as part of normal wear.

Please note that **modifications** to an instrument also will affect an instrument's value (usually downward), and we will deal with such in a separate chapter.

While there are no condition rating guidelines that are "etched in stone" among guitar buffs and vintage shops, it is apparent that the systems that many retailers cite for conditions of instruments in their catalogs or inventory lists is something along the lines of the following list of terms (with definitions accompanying each):

1. "MINT": Looks new; may even have original tags
2. "EXCELLENT": A few minor scratches or dings; very clean
3. "VERY GOOD": Light, normal wear
4. "GOOD": Numerous signs of wear but nevertheless still useful as a utility instrument
5. "FAIR": Outright damage to finish, discoloration, etc. but still playable
6. "POOR": Instrument has several of the nine problems listed previously

Some guitar shops will use terms such as "Very Good" and "Very Good Plus" but it seems that getting that particular only serves to confuse the average person seeking knowledge about his/her instrument. Hopefully these five condition ratings will be sufficient for most readers.

It also goes without saying that all of the electronics should be in working order on electric guitars and basses; instruments should be plugged in and each pickup, volume control and tone control should be checked individually. Any electric problem is probably repairable, but that's extra expense to the ultimate owner. So while problems with an instrument's electronics are a bit harder to figure into its condition rating, nevertheless such problems figure into what dollar amount the instrument may be worth to a prospective seller or buyer (and in the case of pawn shops, **loan amount** would be affected).

This chapter has endeavored to make the reader aware of how certain guitars and basses are considered by most vintage guitar retailers and enthusiasts. Hopefully, using the aforementioned terms and condition rating guidelines will put the average person with an interest in an instrument or instruments that he/she owns on more of the same wave length with such vintage folks, but at the very least these guidelines should give readers a better idea of not only what **kind** of instrument they have in terms of desirability, but also how its condition should affect its desirability.

MODIFICATIONS: IMPROVEMENTS VS. "FRANKENSTEINS"

Almost nothing agitates a guitar buff more than encountering a classic, American-made instrument that has been highly modified to the point that it's a "Frankenstein"; i.e., something that has been "mutated" into a repulsive item. It should go without saying that any instrument, regardless of its age and price point, would be more valuable if it is completely original; **even minor modifications that cannot be reversed will send both the desirability and value of an instrument downward!** Even re-fretting (replacing worn fret wire) can devalue a guitar or bass.

AFTERMARKET PARTS, RETRO-FIT PARTS and PERMANENT MODIFICATIONS

In a column in an issue of Vintage Guitar along this same subject matter, I stated that I was not advocating that all instruments remain in an unmodified state. Beginning in the Seventies, an entire sub-industry began blossoming, making replacement parts for guitars and basses; such "aftermarket" parts were designed to replace less-than-reliable original parts on an instrument.

Examples of better-known replacement parts would be combination bridge/tailpieces and tuning machines. In both cases, the replacement items would provide better tuning reliability than an original bridge/tailpiece or tuning machine would have.

Of course, another example of instrument modifications using aftermarket parts involves pickup replacement with units that will provide a different (and hopefully **improved**) sound on electric guitars and basses. This segment of aftermarket parts offers the widest selection of items from which to choose, and in some cases even active circuitry can be installed as an attempt to improve an instrument's sound.

Pickup replacement, as is the case with most aftermarket parts, can involve either simple "drop-in" replacements or installation where routing has to be done to the body of the instrument; a definitive example would be a humbucking-type pickup replacing a smaller, single-coil unit.

Anytime a replacement part can be installed with no modification to the instrument, the part is referred to as "retro-fit", meaning that it should fit exactly, and the original part could be re-installed to bring an instrument back to its completely original status. This is of course the preferable concept to those who are interested in classic used and vintage American instruments.

So much for replacement parts for original parts; now what about removal of original parts where nothing replaces the original? Examples include pickup covers, bridge/tailpiece covers and pickguards. While removal of such may facilitate easier playing for some individuals, **original parts should be retained**, even if aftermarket/retro-fit parts are not installed as replacements. Missing original parts will devalue an instrument, even if such original parts are lousy. Among the first things guitar buffs will do if they are considering an instrument is to rummage through the guitar's case and/or ask the then-owner about missing original parts. Such inquisitiveness has merit.

Before addressing the final aspect of instrument modification, it seems important to stress that **an instrument should be altered as much as desired if the guitar or bass serves a utilitarian/"workhorse" purpose.** An example cited in the aforementioned <u>Vintage Guitar</u> article was a Sixties Gibson Melody Maker that had had two humbucking pickups installed, replacing its original single-coil pickups. The Melody Maker isn't particularly collectible and was a beginner's instrument when it was in production. On the other hand, the same column also noted a 1936 Gibson L-7 "Advanced Type" archtop guitar that had had two humbucking pickups installed on its surface, along with two volume pots, two tone pots, and a three-way toggle switch. It was quite depressing to encounter this definitive "Frankenstein".

REFINISHING and COSMETICS

The final modification that needs to be considered (especially before proceeding with it) involves an instrument's cosmetics; i.e., something that might make it look better (at least in some persons' eyes), but the instrument's sound isn't affected.

Regardless of whether the reader might be considering doing any type of permanent cosmetic modification to an instrument he/she owns, or the purchase of an instrument that has been permanently altered in its appearance is being considered, the reader needs to be aware that **most vintage authorities and retailers agree that refinishing alone lowers an instrument's dollar value by 1/3 to 1/2!** So while a wild color might look flashy onstage (same goes for custom graphics on an instrument's body), it can really knock down an instrument's desirability and value if the wild color and/or graphics are added in the aftermarket segment and are permanent.

Even stripping off an instrument's finish down to the bare wood and then lacquering it so that it will have a "natural" finish lowers value by the same percentage. Back in the Sixties, the Beatles stripped the finishes off of some of their instruments; George Harrison states that the Epiphone Casinos that were modified this way were not re-lacquered; i.e., the bare wood was left exposed, and Harrison claims that the guitars seemed to "breathe" better. Obviously, such a Beatles-owned Epiphone Casino would fetch a phenomenal amount if it were ever sold, strictly due to the "star power" involved!

In summary, a player should have the freedom to modify his/her instrument in any way he/she desires, but on the flip side, an owner would be well advised to consider doing nothing to an instrument that will alter its original condition permanently if he/she expects to get any sort of deal when it's sold or traded (particularly if it's sold or traded to a vintage shop; trading it in to a music store for another instrument is an entirely different situation, but even music stores will take note of modifications).

"Frankensteins" tend to disgust most vintage buffs, as do "corpses", which are instruments that are in "poor" condition; a definitive example would be the Bicentennial Firebird previously cited. The only modification I've done to one of my instruments over the last few years was to place vinyl, stick-on letters on my practice bass that spell out "DEATH BEFORE DISCO". It's a no-frills, utilitarian instrument, yet even placement of such stick-on cosmetics can affect an instrument's finish, particularly if such cosmetics remain on the instrument for an extended period of time. The guitar of bass may fade in color, but the part of the body under the letters will not fade, which could make for some weird **permanent** cosmetics once the letters are removed! What's more, the glue on such stick-on products may damage the finish. (For the record, I didn't leave the "DEATH BEFORE DISCO" phrase on my practice bass too long, and it was a **white** instrument; obviously white tends to fade less than any other color...)

Please consider all of the factors involved before proceeding with any permanent modifications (or purchasing a modified instrument)!

"WHAT'S IT WORTH?"

Don't ask me! The question concerning the retail value of a guitar or bass is probably heard more often than any other question, including inquiries that in some aspects should be more important (such as the instrument's history). In many ways that's an unfortunate trend, but understandable since interest in classic American-made instruments has been constantly on the increase.

Many guitar buffs rely on appraisals concerning the value of their collections, especially for insurance purposes (just as anyone would do with any item of value). Some of the pawn shops that I have dealt with over the years are set up to do appraisals on gold and jewelry, and many people rely on such appraisals for their gold and jewelry collections.

Yet the first question many of the same shops would ask a vintage enthusiast concerning a particular instrument that might come out of the back for retail sale would be something along the lines of: "How much should that thing sell for?". My standard response to such an inquiry is to state that I don't appraise instruments, since I am not a vintage retailer, but I would be glad to refer them to such a store. Most pawn shops decline to pursue it that far, and in some unfortunate circumstances they've declined to even quote me a price (probably thinking to themselves: "Well, if **he's** interested in it, it must be worth a lot more than I can sell it to him for."). Fortunately, these sorry situations are in a minority, and I resolve to never furnish information to, or deal with, such stores again. I don't believe in stereotyping, but I think that circumstances like these are why pawnbrokers sometimes have a somewhat negative public image. I would emphasize again, however, that most of my dealings with pawn shops are done in a courteous and business-like manner, and information that I provide to pawn shops with which I have a good working relationship gives them additional sales help if I am not interested in the instrument for myself.

IN PRAISE OF APPRAISALS

If anyone has an instrument that he/she feels needs an appraisal, the owner should first consider whether the brand name of the instrument and its country of origin would merit the investment in an appraisal. In general, the more promotional an instrument was when new, the less valuable it is now, despite what its condition might be. If an owner went ahead with an appraisal on a Sixties Harmony guitar, for example, he/she would probably end up disappointed with the appraised amount.

Another reason appraisals should be considered on finer pieces would be fluctuations in the vintage guitar market as noted in this book's introduction. Accordingly, owners might be well advised to get an appraisal **immediately prior to selling it** to get the most accurate value. In some cases a first appraisal should be done to get information about a particular instrument, then a second one should be done if an extended period of time has passed by the time an owner gets ready to sell an instrument, as in most cases the value would have changed (sometimes drastically).

So much for the "in praise of appraisals" concept; what about where to get such appraisals done? Most guitar-oriented periodicals have classified ads for vintage dealers, and most of them do instrument appraisals. It's preferable, of course, if a dealer can examine an instrument first-hand, but appraisals can also be done by mail. In such cases, the vintage retailer would need the following information in order to give the most accurate appraisal:

1. Photos of instrument (front and back)
2. Serial number
3. Location of serial number on instrument
4. Modifications
5. Any signs of damage or wear and tear not visible in photos

Sending the preceding information along with your payment should get you a signed and dated appraisal from the vintage dealer soon thereafter.

Owners of instruments should also consider photographing each guitar or bass in their collections, and placing the negatives and prints, along with the preceding information, in a safe place, like a safety deposit box at a bank, for two important reasons:

1. In case of fire, theft or similar circumstances, an insurance company would need appraisals from qualified authorities before settling any claims on stolen or damaged instruments.

2. According to one guitar authority, the statute of limitations does not expire on instruments if they are stolen, even if the contraband goes out of a particular state. This particular guitar authority had a Rickenbacker instrument stolen from his own collection some years ago, and the serial number is still on file at the Rickenbacker offices in case the company ever receives an inquiry about it.

"BRAND-NAME BOW-WOWS"

Many times a noted instrument maker will market some series of guitars and/or basses that will, to use a common term, "bomb". In some cases, the series has ultimately become quite valuable, such as first edition Gibson Explorers and Flying Vs from 1958; however, the more current unsuccessful styles have been dubbed by some as "brand name bow-wows", for obvious reasons. Such guitars and basses were not only unsuccessful as new instruments, there's just not that much interest in them in the used market as well (most "bow-wows" aren't old enough to merit "vintage" status as of this writing). That's not to say that such instruments will always be maligned; consider the ultimate resurgence in the Danelectro/Silvertone "amp in the case" series. They still don't fetch much in the vintage market, but nevertheless in the late Eighties the going rate for clean examples was still over twice what their original list price was in the Sixties.

Right or wrong, "star power" might also be a factor in whether or not a "bow-wow" might suddenly become desirable (see "As Played By..."), but in spite of that, the following list is relatively accurate in designating instruments that just don't command that much attention in both the desirability and value areas, at least for now. While this might be the most opinionated and controversial section of the book, most other vintage retailers and buffs would probably agree that the instruments listed deserve their "bow-wow" designation:

ANY GIBSON INSTRUMENT WITH A BOLT-ON NECK: Indicates a lower-priced instrument when compared to other Gibsons. Examples include:

GUITARS	BASSES
S-1	Grabber
Marauder	G-3
L-6 Deluxe	Victory
Corvus	
Invader	
Challenger	

GIBSON INSTRUMENTS WITH MAPLE FRETBOARDS AND PEARL DOT FRET MARKERS: Many of the instruments in the preceding list also fall into this category, but some other instruments from the mid-to-late Seventies (when this dumb cosmetic idea was applied) had hard-to-see pearl dots on maple fretboards. Other examples include the Ripper bass, the L-6S guitar and RD series guitars and basses. For that matter, the Ripper and L-6S don't fetch much in any finish (same goes for RDs, listed separately).

GIBSON RD SERIES: Due to cosmetics as well as confusion over their "Artist" active circuitry. May have been ahead of their time regarding active electronics, but they were duds in terms of sales, and still are. Other Gibson body styles had "Artist" active circuitry put into them (most likely to use up leftover circuit boards), but these aren't necessarily in demand either.

FENDER "LEAD" SERIES: A solidbody group from the early Eighties that didn't catch on.

FENDER "CORONADO" GUITARS AND BASSES: Fender's thin-line electrics have never sold well; apparently the company has always had a solidbody "surf guitar" stereotype among players. The follow-up "Antigua" series was comprised of Coronado guitars in the ghost-like Antigua finish, which can also be found on other Fender instruments; Antigua-finished Coronados would be somewhat more desirable and/or valuable, in the opinion of most guitar buffs.

ANY SHORT-SCALE BASS GUITAR: For reasons described in the "Guitar-ology 101" chapter. Exceptions would of course include high-end, custom-made units, but the likes of Fender's Musicmaster and Gibson's "EB" series are not as sought-after in the used/vintage market as are full-scale instruments of the same brand and/or time period.

RICKENBACKER GUITARS WITH BOLT-ON NECKS: For the same reasons as Gibsons with bolt-on necks.

GRETSCH GUITARS WITH BOLT-ON NECKS: Again, the same rationale applies here as with Gibson and Rickenbacker, but a Gretsch with a bolt-on neck is probably one that was "hecho en Mexico" to boot. However, some Mexican Gretsches may have glued-on necks or even neck-through construction, so don't be fooled.

BUDGET/PROMOTIONAL MODELS BY A MAJOR MANUFACTURER: Any guitar or bass that was a budget instrument back in its time is usually lower-priced in the vintage mart. Examples include Fender's Mustang and Gibson's Melody Maker.

RICKENBACKER GUITARS WITH SLANTED FRETS: An idea that was supposed to make for more comfortable playing; however, the instruments looked lopsided, and such aesthetics contributed to a significant lack of interest then and now.

ALMOST ALL SINGLE-PICKUP GUITARS: Due to the limit of tonal capability, most single-pickup guitars usually do not interest serious players or collectors, and such instruments tend to be oriented towards casual players and/or beginners. Therefore, a large percentage of promotional models by major manufacturers are/were single-pickup types. However, there **are** some exceptions such as the Dan Armstrong/Ampeg "See Through" series of guitars and basses, or virtually any electric hollow body guitar (such as the Gibson ES-175) which many jazz players prefer with a single pickup over a double (D) version.

Bass guitars are slightly different when it comes to models with one pickup; the Fender Precision has always had a solitary pickup, and it's always been the world's most popular electric bass. More pickups means more sound capability, of course, but it can make an instrument worth more if it's used or vintage. However, three pickup models don't automatically fetch 1 1/2 times what two pickup models would, so don't think that "more pickups" means "more value".

Of course, it also goes without saying that "sub-brands", "house brands" and lines made overseas under name licensing are not as valuable, and these types are covered in detail in a separate chapter.

Perhaps the most polite thing that one could say about many of the preceding models and styles is that in some cases they may have been "ahead of their time" and/or "underrated". While such descriptions may seem like clichés to some, in some situations it's difficult to try to assign a dollar value to **any** instrument if there's a lot of "sentimental value" involved (quite frankly, "sentimental value" may be yet another cliché to business people, but to many players the idea has merit). Many vintage enthusiasts have heard players state that they wouldn't get rid of their instrument "for all the money in the world", and that can't help but be respected, although it would be interesting to attempt some kind of survey to determine how many of the same players ended up pawning or selling the same instrument.

As noted in the "Terms and Conditions" chapter, someone may want to buy an instrument for one of three reasons (or combinations of these three reasons): To play, to collect or to sell or trade off later. Some pawn shops claim that they will quote prices a bit differently if they can determine for what purpose a prospective buyer is considering an instrument. This is at best somewhat disturbing, at worst it's discriminatory. If an instrument is sold, it's technically none of the previous owner's business what the new owner does with it, and this rationale can apply not only to pawn shops but to other businesses such as flea markets and private owners as well. Fortunately, such sorry circumstances are in the vast minority of most used guitar deals, but there's still no excuse for such behavior by a prospective seller.

So hopefully the reader has been aware of the fact that much of the dollar value cited by owners of used instruments should be investigated through appraisals; the importance of appraisals has been stressed in other sections of this book as well. What's more, the "bow-wows" cited may help a business or individual from getting stuck with such an instrument, whereby an incident such as the following could be avoided:

The affable pawn shop owner had just pulled a Rickenbacker model 481 out of the back; this model was one of Rickenbacker's slanted frets types. "Yeah, the guy that pawned this tol' me it cost him eighteen hunnert dollars", he stated.

"Uh, did you believe him?!?" was my incredulous response. The shop owner could tell by the tone of my voice that something was wrong, and his next action was to inquire as to how much it was worth.

I didn't give him a price figure, but I let him know when it was made, how many years the model was made, etc. I didn't ask him how much he'd loaned on it, because that was none of my business; suffice to say that **his** tone of voice seemed to indicate he may have loaned a bit more than he should have.

Ultimately I purchased another instrument from this store, and he gets in touch whenever he needs information or has something he thinks I might be interested in. He still usually asks how much something is worth, knowing full well I won't appraise his instrument, but if he and I can both be happy with the circumstances, then everyone comes out ahead.

"AS PLAYED BY . . . . . "

The Missus has on occasion accused yours truly of being somewhat ambivalent at times. *"Don't you think that sometimes you're kind of wishy-washy about some things?"* she'll ask.

My response is a firm, unequivocal: "Well... yes and no..."

That pretty much sums up how many guitar enthusiasts feel about the concept of "star power" and/or endorsements of particular models and brands by famous players. In some cases, **talent** has absolutely nothing to do with whether a guitarist or bassist endorses a particular instrument; he/she just happens to be in a band that's popular at the time.

In some cases, the same performer will endorse brands of instruments, amplifiers, devices and strings! Not only that, but one particular bassist has lent his moniker to **three** different brands of bass guitars over the years!

Obviously, the term "sell-out" could come into play here; endorsements can be controversial enough, but when very talented individuals get overlooked not only in the musical mainstream but in the endorsement field as well, it's doubly unfortunate; someone who just happens to be a bigger "star" can help a guitar company sell more instruments, even if a lesser-known player who happens to use the same equipment could blow the so-called "star" off the stage.

That's not to say that lesser-known players with superior talent go completely unrecognized, however. There are many examples in the guitar field of "player's players"; individuals who are well known by musicians themselves if not by the general public. In such cases, endorsement ads may appear in the likes of Guitar Player and Guitar World featuring such "player's players". In other cases, however, the circumstances can involve a relatively obscure player **as well as** a relatively obscure brand name, so who knows if the individual is a "player's player" or not?

Some artists will not endorse instruments or equipment at all, although technically if they play a particular model for an extended period of time, it's an "unadvertised endorsement"; the example most often cited is Jimi Hendrix and Fender Stratocasters.

Other artists change brands and models quite often. Nowadays some players use several different instruments during a single concert and have their own "guitar technicians" to maintain their wide array of guitars or basses.

Over the years, some artists that have remained pretty much in the public eye have gone through so many brands it's quite difficult to state that he/she uses a certain type of guitar or bass. For example, Pete Townshend of the Who has used the following brands and models of guitars in his musical ventures since the Sixties: Fender Jazzmaster, Fender Electric XII, Fender Stratocaster, Fender Telecaster, Gibson Les Paul Deluxe, Gibson SG Special, Schecter Tele-style and several Rickenbacker models. Apparently, the only time Townshend ever got involved with an endorsement was the Rickenbacker "Pete Townshend Limited Edition" in 1987.

In some cases, the artist who endorses a particular model will have had some amount of input into the model's development, particularly if the instrument is a "signature model" or "limited edition" named after the individual. While that's all well and good, as a general rule the endorser probably has a lot of "star power" going for him/her already. There **are** exceptions to minimal player involvement in instrument development, however. For example, bassist Anthony Jackson has been working with more than one manufacturer in developing a six-string "contrabass" for years, yet he's virtually unknown by name in popular music. He **is,** of course, a definitive example of a "player's player".

It's impossible to compile a complete list of famous players and their instruments (regardless of whether or not said instruments are endorsement models), so what follows is listing performers who play them. Also noted by some models will be certain "player's player"; these will be abbreviated as "PPs". Naturally, "signature model" instruments such as the Eric Clapton Stratocaster by Fender and the Rudy Sarzo bass by Peavey will not be listed, but a model that may have been simply **endorsed** by a particular performer may be noted. No individual artist will be cited more than three times, and in most cases the band with which the player has been associated will be noted in parentheses. Year models of guitars or basses will not be specified, nor will any modifications to a specific artist's instrument; let's keep this as simple as possible!

Another factor that needs to be remembered is that **an attempt has been made here to "zero in" on instruments that have been used by these artists for recording or performance purposes only!** Instruments that might happen to be found in a famous musician's own guitar collection will not be noted, nor will guitars or basses that might appear with a musician/star in a music video.

ALEMBIC: Basses: John Entwistle (Who), Mark King (Level 42) PPs: Stanley Clarke, Jimmy Johnson.

AMPEG/DAN ARMSTRONG "See Through": Keith Richard (Rolling Stones), Leslie West (Mountain).

BEAN, TRAVIS: Guitar PP: Stanley Jordan. Bass: Bill Wyman (Rolling Stones).

CARVIN: Craig Chaquico (Starship), Vicki Peterson (Bangles).

DANELECTRO: Jimmy Page (Led Zeppelin, Firm).

DEAN: Elliot Easton (Cars), Rick Ocasek (Cars), John McFee (Doobie Brothers).

FENDER TELECASTER: Bruce Springsteen, Keith Richard. PPs: Scotty Anderson, Albert Lee, Roy Buchanan, Danny Gatton.

FENDER STRATOCASTER: Jimi Hendrix, Eric Clapton, Robin Trower, Jeff Beck, David Gilmour (Pink Floyd) and many others.

FENDER CUSTOM TELECASTER: Andy Summers (Police).

FENDER JAZZMASTER: Elvis Costello.

FENDER JAGUAR: Assorted surf groups.

FENDER MUSTANG: Johnny Winter.

FENDER PRECISION BASS: Almost every bass player in the world has played a Precision professionally at one time.

FENDER JAZZ BASS: About the same as the Precision, except that some players of note include Anthony Jackson, Mark Egan (Pat Metheny Group) and other PPs.

FODERA: Bass: Anthony Jackson.

FRITZ BROTHERS: Jody Payne (Willie Nelson Band), Brad Whitford (Aerosmith). PP: Scotty Anderson.

GIBSON BYRDLAND: Hank Garland, Bill Byrd, Ted Nugent.

GIBSON ES-5: Carl Perkins, Steve Howe (Yes).

GIBSON ES-350: Chuck Berry.

GIBSON LES PAUL CUSTOM: Jeff Beck, Joe Perry (Aerosmith) and many others.

GIBSON LES PAUL STANDARD: Jimmy Page (Led Zeppelin), Eric Clapton, Mark Knopfler (Dire Straits).

GIBSON LES PAUL SPECIAL: Bran Whitford (Aerosmith), Mickey Baker (Mickey & Sylvia).

GIBSON LES PAUL JR.: Leslie West.

GIBSON THIN-LINE SEMI-SOLIDS: B.B. King, Larry Carlton, Alvin Lee (Ten Years After).

GIBSON FLYING V: Albert King, Billy Gibbons (Z.Z. Top), Andy Powell (Wishbone Ash), Lonnie Mack.

GIBSON EXPLORER: Eric Clapton, Billy Gibbons, Tommy Shaw (Styx).

GIBSON FIREBIRD: Johnny Winter, Roland Orzabal (Tears for Fears).

GIBSON SG STANDARD: John Cippolina (Quicksilver Messenger Service), Angus Young (AC/DC).

GIBSON SG SPECIAL: Carlos Santana, Pete Townshend.

GIBSON EB-3 bass: Jack Bruce (Cream).

GRETSCH 6120: Brian Setzer (Stray Cats), Eddie Cochran.

GRETSCH WHITE FALCON: Neil Young, Stephen Stills.

GRETSCH SILVER JET: Joe Perry (Aerosmith).

HAMER: Guitars: Rick Nielsen (Cheap Trick). Basses: Jack Blades (Night Ranger, Damn Yankees).

JACKSON: Randy Rhoads (Ozzy Osbourne), other heavy metal guitarists.

KRAMER: Eddie Van Halen.

KUBICKI, PHILLIP: Bass PPs: Stuart Hamm, Vail Johnson (Kenny G. Band)

MARTIN: Most famous acoustic artists have used Martin instruments.

MESSENGER: Mark Farner (Grand Funk R.R.).

MICRO-FRETS: Mark Farner.

MODULUS GRAPHITE: Bob Weir (Grateful Dead), Bass: Phil Lesh (Grateful Dead).

MOSRITE: The Ventures, and other surf groups.

MUSIC MAN: Bass: Tom Hamilton (Aerosmith).

NATIONAL: Bob Dylan.

OVATION: Glen Campbell.

PEAVEY: Many performers in the Country & Western and Contemporary Christian areas of popular music use Peavey instruments.

PEDULLA, M.V.: Bass PP: Mark Egan.

PENSA-SUHR: Lou Reed, Mark Knofler.

RICH, B.C.: Many heavy metal artists.

RICKENBACKER: Guitars: Roger McGuinn (Byrds), Tom Petty, Pete Townshend, Peter Buck (R.E.M.). Basses: Chris Squire (Yes), Paul McCartney, Lemmy Kilmister (Motorhead). NOTE: McGuinn and Townshend used "Ricks" for many years before endorsing specific models named after them.

SMITH, PAUL REED: Carlos Santana, Ted Nugent.

SPECTOR: Basses: Sting, Greg Lake.

STEINBERGER: Eddie Van Halen. PP: Alan Holdsworth, Michale Hedges
    Basses: Sting, Greg Lake.

TURNER: Lindsay Buckingham.

VALLEY ARTS: Larry Carlton.

Obviously, this list **barely scratches the surface** when it comes to "who plays what", but if nothing else it may serve to "tease" the reader into taking note what some of his/her favorite players might use, and knowing such specific brands and models might help to turn an instrument quicker in a sale situation.

Fans of acoustic players would also probably tend to be miffed that the list doesn't really cite such artists, but unfortunately pop/rock artists who play electric instruments are the most widely known and listened to, so that's the segment from which most instruments manufacturers will seek endorsements.

So while endorsements and "star power" may be controversial, **the "concepts" should be of minimal importance to any player,** regardless of whether a player is a professional musician or one that plays around his/her home for the simple enjoyment of it. If it sounds good and is comfortable to play, who cares who else plays one like it?

20th Century Guitar

COUNTERFEITS and FORGERIES: A GROWING PROBLEM

"Willie, next time you're in the area, stop by my store. I just got a Gibson bass out of the back and I thought you might be interested in it." So said the message left on my answering machine by the owner of a pawn shop about 150 miles from my hometown. I'd bought several instruments from him in the past, and I always poked my head in his store whenever I was in that neck of the woods. Even if he had something that was American-made that I **wasn't** interested in, I'd give him some information about the instrument so he could hopefully sell it quicker to someone else, and he'd reciprocate by selling me instruments that I **was** interested in at a good price; i.e., this was a definitive example of the good business relationship I'd developed with many pawn shops.

Imagine then my disappointment to have to tell the pawn shop owner that his so-called Gibson bass was as phony as a three dollar bill. It looked nothing like any Gibson bass ever produced; in fact, it looked more like a Fender Precision, and it had a phony Gibson decal on the headstock.

I'm aware that many pawn shops have to be on their toes concerning such items as fake Rolex watches, but the number of phony American brand name guitars and basses seems to be on the increase whenever I travel. It seems that the vast majority of these bogus instruments that I've encountered are located in pawn shops that are near military bases; the implication being that some naive airman or seaman may have bought an instrument overseas and relinquished it once he/she came back to the U.S. A good number of them tend to be located along the U.S. coastline as well, so there's also the possibility that such fakes can be brought into the country through commercial shipping employees.

There's gotten to be such an abundance of these phony guitars and basses that it's possible to divide them into two distinct categories, "counterfeits" and "forgeries", even though the terms are somewhat synonymous.

A "counterfeit" instrument would have originally started out as one of the myriad of imported copies of a famous American instrument such as a Gibson Les Paul or a Fender Stratocaster, with a different brand name on the headstock. Such brand names include Cort, Hondo, Bentley, Electra and even names that once belonged to American guitars, such as Harmony; i.e., the last example is an originally American brand name that is now licensed overseas, **found on a copy of another brand name's model.** In the case of a counterfeit, however, the imported name has been scraped off or painted over, and a phony name has been placed on the headstock; usually the fake brand name is Gibson or Fender, but I've even seen a counterfeit Peavey!

The bogus brand name is usually a decal or a screen-printed logo, although occasionally some logos have been seen where some doofus actually **hand-painted** them on the headstock! "Forgeries", on the other hand, apparently come in from overseas as a completely new, ready-to-sell instrument (or as may have been the case with someone in the military, the instrument could have been bought overseas completely new and unaltered). At any rate, most of these forgeries rarely resemble any model of the bogus brand that's on their headstocks, except in a very general way. Again, most of the phony names found on the headstocks of forgeries say "Gibson" or "Fender", as is the case with counterfeits.

A final type of bogus American model guitar would be one that also looks like its American counterpart to boot, right down to the phony headstock logo. A knowledgeable guitar buff can still usually spot better fakes such as these (such instruments would be considered as "counterfeits" instead of "forgeries"). Examples of such intentionally-produced counterfeits include so-called Fender Jaguars that were made in 1964. A so-called Fender Stratocaster shown in the Photo Section's "Rogues' Gallery" is a definitive example of a better-caliber counterfeit.

LEGITIMATE GIBSON and FENDER HEADSTOCK LOGOS

Since Gibson and Fender are the two brand names that are almost always found on the headstocks of fake instruments, it seems appropriate at this point to review the cosmetics of **real** Gibson and Fender logos:

Gibson logos should be in a continuous "script" style, and should be **one color,** either gold, black or pearl. Most of the time the headstock should be a black or natural wood-tone color. There are some exceptions to these general guidelines, however. For example, the 1980 "Firebrand" series of promotional instruments had Gibson logos that were simply **embossed** (pressed) into their headstocks; apparently this idea had something to do with the name of the series, as the names were "branded" and not colored the usual gold or black. Examples of Gibson instruments without a black or natural wood-tone headstock color include the early Seventies SG100, SG200 and SG250.

Fender logos should be just the reverse of Gibson logos; most Fender names on headstocks are **two-tone**; most are also decals while most Gibson logos are screen-printed. Two-tone Fender logos should be either black-and-gold or black-and-silver. The **outline** and the **inside color** can appear in either combination of the two color schemes, so four combinations are possible: Gold with black outline (usually found on Fifties Stratocasters and Jazzmasters, as well as on almost all Fender instruments made in the Sixties), silver with black outline (most Fifties Telecasters and Precisions, as well as most Eighties instruments), black with gold outline (most Seventies instruments) and black with silver outline (Eighties instruments).

Exceptions to the above general guidelines include the jazz-type Fenders, which had pearl logos, as well as Fender acoustic guitars made by Harmony, which generally had a one-color white logo. There may have been other exceptions as well.

Another Fender tip is the fact that genuine Fender instruments will almost always have the model's name on the headstock, right by the Fender logo. The Swinger/Musiclander/"Arrow" is an exception to this guideline; the only name seen by its Fender logo was "Swinger", and it was not found on all instruments of this model.

Examples of phony Gibson and Fender logos encountered by the author have included the following:
--A one-color silver "Fender Stratocaster" logo (as well as a serial number!) screen-printed onto the headstock of an imported Stratocaster copy.
--A black "Gibson" logo with a gold border that resembled a real Gibson name, except the letters were separate from each other and were not in a "script" style.
--A gold "Fender" logo that was an outline only; the color of the instrument's headstock showed through the middle of the logo (in this case, the color was royal blue, and matched the instrument's body). There was also a tiny gold "registration" mark by the "Fender" logo, as well as "Stratocaster" in small gold letters. Unfortunately, all of the above was on a **bass guitar**; there is no such thing as a Fender Stratocaster bass.
--Numerous instruments with **phony decals** on them; sometimes **decals only** will be advertised and sold here in the U.S.! If someone tries to pass off a phony instrument as a legitimate brand name by using such a decal, it's bad enough, but sometimes an unscrupulous owner will try to pass off a newer Fender instrument as an older model by subbing a "spaghetti" logo decal for a more current style.

Fender authentication can get more complicated, since their vintage re-issue instruments (both domestic and imported) use the "spaghetti" logo as well!

While examining headstock logos to help authenticate instruments is quite helpful, perhaps the easiest way to quickly determine if an instrument is a possible phony is to note the serial number, **if there is one. Most of the time, any instrument with a popular American brand name that does not have a serial number is a fake!** Such was the case with all of the instruments previously cited as phonies, with the exception of the "Fender Stratocaster" with the one-color screen print logo.

Admittedly, in some cases a serial number may be missing (such as a label that may have been in an acoustic or electric-acoustic instrument), but no serial number should make a prospective recipient of an instrument very skittish, regardless of whether the proposed transaction is a sale or pawn loan! If the instrument does have a legitimate serial number, it can of course be dated much more easily.

The unscrupulous persons who manufacture bogus instruments are apparently getting better at their craft, as in the summer of 1990 the author came across an unbelievably accurate counterfeit of a Fender Stratocaster (as the Stratocaster is the world's most popular model, more and more counterfeits and forgeries of it are appearing these days). There were some minor cosmetic incongruities that would probably be noticeable only to a guitar buff. Such cosmetic anomalies were a black logo with a **yellow gold border instead of a normal 'old gold' border**, different and cheaper tuning keys, and the word "STRATOCASTER" appeared to have been placed on the headstock one letter at a time; the letters were a bit irregular in their lineup. Another giveaway was the bell-shaped truss rod cover on the headstock; real Stratocasters have never had a truss rod system that involved a cover on the headstock. This counterfeit had a serial number that bore an uncanny resemblance to a Seventies number; the instrument was so realistic it probably would fool any pawn shop or casual player that saw it, unless a pawn shop employee or player really knew his/her instruments.

Hopefully this chapter will prevent too many folks from getting stuck with something that's bogus. Counterfeits and forgeries of American guitars and basses haven't gotten to the "epidemic" status of the aforementioned Rolex watches (in fact, it's my understanding that there are **countless** counterfeits of Stradivarius violins around; I've seen many of those as well), but bogus Fender Stratocasters and Gibson Les Pauls seem to be popping up with an ever-increasing frequency, and I don't like having to disappoint people by telling them that what they have is technically worthless. It's a sad situation that will hopefully improve someday, but I'm not optimistic.

WHEELING AND DEALING:
PAWN SHOPS, PRIVATE OWNERS, MANUFACTURERS, VINTAGE RETAILERS, GUITAR COLLECTORS and GUITAR ENTHUSIASTS

This chapter will consist primarily of opinion based on experience, and it may be the most controversial of all the chapters in the book. It is primarily directed at stores (the vast majority of which would be pawn shops) and individuals that might be interested in selling a guitar or bass, and also to such owners of instruments that might decide to seek detailed information about an instrument, whether they are planning on selling it or not.

Getting an appraisal for your instrument has been encouraged at several points throughout the text. If you plan on selling it, it would be a smart move to **get a current, dated appraisal** on your instrument even if it's been previously appraised; remember that the vintage market can be quite unstable, price-wise. An updated appraisal is an important first step, particularly if the instrument to be sold is a well-known brand name and/or the instrument if obviously a higher-end, well-crafted piece. However, to what extent the expenditure for appraisals on items such as Silvertone/Danelectro guitars would be worthwhile is debatable.

If, on the other hand, you are wanting to know only what the model and year of manufacture of your instrument is, some vintage shops will still identify it. A photo of the instrument and its serial number should be mailed to the vintage retailer, **along with a stamped, self-addressed envelope for its return.** Addresses of vintage stores can of course be found in the classified sections of such publications as Vintage Guitar (which also has half-page and quarter-page ads by vintage shops as well), Guitar Player , Guitar World , 20th Century Guitar and Acoustic Guitar.

Remember that if you do not opt to invest in an appraisal, a vintage retailer is under no obligation whatsoever to even respond to a letter of inquiry if there's no stamped, self-addressed envelope accompanying it.

Phone calls to vintage stores might also get some kind of response, but the information might be less reliable since the retailer can't examine a photograph of an instrument.

Inquiries for information only should not even **hint** at wanting to know how much an instrument is worth. One successful vintage retailer claims that his store gets **five hundred calls per day**, and that if anyone asks for even a "ballpark" figure (either by mail **or** phone) without investing in an appraisal, the shop's response is "Cubs vs. Pirates, Wrigley Field, July 26th, 8-3".

An alternative to contacting a vintage retailer would be to contact a manufacturer itself (if the factory is still in business, which many times isn't the case); some guitar manufacturers have a company historian, or at least an individual who is designated to respond to inquiries from the general public. Again, the best procedure to follow would be to send a photograph along with pertinent information, plus a stamped, self-addressed envelope. About the only dollar figure a factory representative should be expected to furnish is what the list price of the instrument would have been when it was made. The best place to find company addresses is in guitar magazines.

There is an obvious difference between a vintage retailer and a vintage collector; the former is a **business** and the latter is a consumer that usually does business with the former. In some retail situations (usually pawn shops), a store owner may have trouble in distinguishing between the two, and sometimes that makes for unfortunate circumstances for everyone concerned if there's no transaction completed where everyone could come out ahead.

Some sorry situations have been noted elsewhere in this book: The pawn shop that refused to quote me a price on instruments (apparently figuring that since I was interested in them, said instruments were probably valuable), the pawn shops that won't negotiate or quote a cash price if they suspect a potential customer might also be able to sell an instrument for a higher price, etc.

It's the opinion of most guitar enthusiasts that most pawn shops deal with musical instruments primarily because they **have to;** apparently the bread-and-butter items for many pawn shops are gold, diamonds and guns, and such shops know little about guitars and basses (except they think a Gibson or Fender should fetch more). Many shops rely on price-oriented musical instrument books (that are updated annually and cost about a hundred dollars per year). Such books offer little information other than price only, which can cause a lot of misunderstanding if a pawn shop is not aware of an instrument's condition, modifications, etc., or whether or not the instrument is a fake.

A general stereotype of a guitar enthusiast (who may also be a vintage retailer **and/or** collector) is that he/she would probably be more clean-cut and affable than most **musicians** that would enter a pawn shop seeking to pawn or sell an instrument. The "plus" about guitar buffs is that they can offer accurate information to pawn shops **if** the pawn shops choose to reciprocate by offering good deals. The "negative" can be that one of the two parties can be too abrasive: Either the guitar buff can come on too strong ("I'll give ya $_____! I've got the cash money right here, right now!"), or as previously noted, the pawn shop won't cooperate with someone who is apparently quite interested in an instrument and seems to know what he/she is talking about.

It would probably make everyone more content if such transactions could be handled in a smooth, business-like manner, but regrettably that's not always the case. If either party chooses to erect some kind of barrier to completing a transaction suitable to both buyer and seller, both lose.

There are plenty of vintage retailers throughout the U.S., and there are also enough people interested in vintage guitars that almost any area of the country tends to have a local/regional collector or enthusiast. If you've decided to actually sell an instrument, there are important points to remember when dealing with either retailers or individuals (regardless of whether you the seller is a business or an individual):

Most vintage retailers will accept instruments on consignment to be sold for a percentage of the retail price. What vintage retailers can offer a consignor is not only display of the instrument in a vintage store, but most shops will also place the guitar or bass on their inventory list, which is usually published monthly and mailed to subscribers.

When consigning an instrument to a vintage retailer, the documentation should involve a total of **four dollar figures**: An "advertised" price, a lower "sell for" price and the division of this lower retail price between the store and the consignor.

In some cases, vintage retailer consignment forms will have an alternate or optional type of documentation, with a figure that simply states how much the consignor wants to get out of his/her instrument. In this case, the vintage retailer is allowed a bit more flexibility. The consigned instrument may be traded by the retailer, or sold in some "package" deal involving several instruments; under the terms of the first type of consignment agreement, such actions would not be possible. In most cases, the instrument would probably sell faster if the latter type of consignment is done, and once the instrument has been turned, the consignor would receive the aforementioned singular dollar amount.

Owners of quality instruments need to be advised that most of the time, any vintage dealer that is a good businessperson will inquire if a prospective consignor wishes to sell an instrument to his/her shop outright. Most of the better vintage retailers advertise that they pay cash for used American instruments in good condition, so be prepared to either negotiate or decline.

Should an instrument's owner ultimately consider a direct sale to a vintage store, it goes without saying that the owner should not expect to receive an instrument's appraised value, if an appraisal has been done. A more common situation that is similar to such a scenario would involve someone trading in or selling a used car. If, on the other hand, the owner of an older instrument decides to contact a local/regional guitar collector or enthusiast, the collector/enthusiast **may or may not be interested in purchasing your instrument, and may immediately refer you to a vintage store.** Some guitar buffs will furnish **information only,** and if such a guitar buff is not also a vintage retailer, he/she should not be asked to appraise an instrument.

Such a local/regional guitar enthusiast/collector could possibly be located only by word of mouth, and perhaps a local musical instrument store could offer a referral. Of course, many musical instrument stores may have an employee that is a guitar buff himself/herself, and perhaps the information sought could be obtained right there!

If a guitar enthusiast/collector that does **not** work in a musical instrument store expresses an interest in purchasing an instrument, it can be handled between the owner and enthusiast/collector as a private sale; it would be nice to think that owners would give a good deal to someone who is interested in a guitar or bass because of the instrument's history, craftsmanship, etc. Of course, the guitar enthusiast/collector has every right to sell or trade the instrument sometime down the road, but subsequent owners of classic guitars and basses would most likely also be individuals who are interested in caring for such instruments.

So whether you're a pawn shop or some other retail venture such as a flea market that happens to have a used guitar, or if you're an individual who's finally planning on getting rid of an instrument, you should know that there are procedures whereby owners of used guitars or basses can hopefully get the kind of information they need, so that hopefully they can get their best deal **and** satisfy the purchaser with a good deal as well, regardless if the purchaser is a vintage retailer or an individual.

There are a lot of people who are interested in American instruments, for a variety of reasons. Courteous dealings with such guitar buffs can make everyone a winner. There's room for everyone, so let's make it work!

USEFUL TIPS:
(PRIMARILY FOR PAWNBROKERS)

DATING ELECTRIC GUITARS WHEN THERE'S NO SERIAL NUMBER (OR A SERIAL NUMBER DOESN'T HELP): Many of the books cited in the Bibliography have serial number listings with dating codes for some of the more popular brands of American guitars; moreover, a new anthology of serial numbers of American instruments is also in the works as of this writing (this will be addressed in the "Outro" section).

However, what is someone to do when a guitar doesn't have a serial number (Danelectros, for example), and/or the American company has gone out of business? Another problem in dating instruments involves an American company that still might be in business, but at certain times in the company's history their serial numbering system (if any) wasn't exactly precise (Gibson is the difinitive example in this circumstance).

A tremendous step in dating American-made electric guitars was announced in the October 1990 issue of Guitar Player magazine. Written by George Gruhn and Walter Carter, the article described the research efforts of Hans Moust, a Dutch guitar dealer and collector. Mr. Moust has ascertained that the potentiometers ("pots") on American-made instruments should be **coded as to the year, and even the week that the pot was made.** This coding system was developed by Electronic Industries Association, and is of course applicable to pots found in amplifiers as well as guitars. Obviously, dating acoustic instruments isn't helped by this "new" system, which really isn't new at all.

The E.I.A. coding system has been in effect since the late Forties, and involves numbers that are stamped onto the housing of each potentiometer, so the "guts" of each instrument would need to be examined. In the case of some instruments, such as Gibson Les Pauls or SGs, looking into the guitar would simply involve removing the plate on the back of the instrument. In the case of instruments that have controls installed in a flush-mounted pickguard (Fender, Danelectro), the guitar's strings would need to be de-tuned and the pickguard removed, The largest amount of patience and elbow grease would be required in dating arch-top electrics; controls would need to be extricated through existing pickup holes or f-holes.

The numbering system of the code involves either six digits (1947-1959) or seven digits (1960 to present). In either case, **the first three digits of the code represent a specific manufacturer of the potentiometer.** For example, the number 137 stands for a company known as CTS, and as it is found on a large number of pots, it will be the number cited in the following examples.

```
SIX DIGIT CODE (1947-1959)  EXAMPLE:  137610
137    =       manufacturer's code number
6      =       last digit of year pot was made
10     =       week of year pot was made
```

This particular potentiometer was made by CTS in the **10**th week of 195**6** (March 1956).

Obviously, there would be some overlap in this coding system for the years 1947, 1948 and 1949 and their Fifties counterparts, 1957, 1958 and 1959, and some 1960 numbers may have six digits instead of seven. However, most electric guitars will have other clues as to whether they're late Forties or late Fifties models, so this overlap isn't much of a problem to most guitar enthusiasts.

```
SEVEN DIGIT CODE (1960 to present)  EXAMPLE:  1376610
137    =       manufacturer's code number
66     =       year pot was made
10     =       week of year pot was made
```

This particular potentiometer was made by CTS in the **10**th week of 19**66** (March 1966).

It's a fairly simple system, but there are several important things to remember when using this system to date electric guitars:

1. The number may be found on either side or back of the pot.

2. Some manufacturer's code numbers may have one or two digits instead of three, which could throw an observer off course. In some cases the manufacturers did not have room for all six or seven digits, so be careful!

3. Remember that it's possible that a replacement pot or pots may have been installed; in such cases an instrument would possibly be dated as younger than it actually may be. One hint in avoiding this "trap" is to look for newer, brighter gobs of solder where the pots have been installed; if such is the case, such pots are probably replacements.

4. There may be a hyphen between the manufacturer's code number and the rest of the number (for example, 137-6610).

Above all, the most important thing to remember about the E.I.A. pot code dating system is that this system concerns the date that potentiometers were made and not necessarily guitars themselves! It stands to reason that any pot made in the latter weeks of a given year probably ended up on an electric guitar that was assembled the next year. Moreover, in many cases certain guitar companies bought potentiometers in huge quantities, and some pots may not have been used in production for several years! The author once encountered a budget Gibson instrument that was only made by the company for a short time (circa 1971), but it had original potentiometers in it that were made in 1966!

While some effort may be required in examining the controls on an electric guitar in an attempt to apply the E.I.A. code system, it can nevertheless make for some useful information that may make such an effort worthwhile. When in doubt, however, a vintage retailer or guitar buff should be contacted to help with authentication.

THE DRACULA SYNDROME: Remember the legend about how vampires can't stand sunlight? Well, neither can fretted instruments. Exposure to sunlight and heat can cause the finish of an instrument to fade, crack, blister or peel (or any combination of the preceding maladies). Heat (whether generated by exposure to sunlight or from another source) can also cause warpage, particularly on acoustic instruments. If you happen to have a store, don't display an instrument in a window that gets direct sunlight!

DE-TUNE DAT SUCKAH!: The most common example of fretted instrument neglect is a warped neck. Usually neck bowing a attributable to a guitar or bass remaining in a tuned-but-unplayed state for an extended period of time, whether the instrument is on display in a store or in storage. It is recommended that instruments that are going to be stored or taken in for pawn by pawn shops be de-tuned; i.e., the strings should be loosened to the point that they do not make a musical note when plucked or strummed. In fact, a pawn shop should recommend de-tuning to a customer who is pawning an instrument.

In most cases a warped neck can be corrected by adjusting the truss rod, but as previously noted, this type of adjustment should only be done by a qualified guitar technician. In cases of severe neck warpage, many guitar stores have a sort of heat press that requires leaving the instrument at the store overnight (and this can run into some expense). The old "ounce of prevention" proverb is definitely applicable to a guitar neck, so consider loosening the instrument's strings if it won't be played for awhile.

Another "plus" for displaying an out-of-pawn instrument in a de-tuned state is that it gives a pawn shop employee a chance to determine if a prospective customer knows what he/she is talking about when he/she is examining an instrument. One of the first things a knowledgeable customer will do will be to "sight" the neck length-wise to check for warpage; what's more, if a potential customer can't tune up a de-tuned instrument, that ought to tell you something right there…

THE CASE FOR CASES: To most musicians, buying a quality guitar or bass (or any other instrument, for that matter) **and not getting a case for it** is somewhat akin to buying an automobile without a roof; i.e., it'll get you where you're going, but you'll have a lot less protection.

In most cases (no pun intended), if an older instrument that is in good shape also happens to have its original case, that should add to the retail value, particularly if the case itself is in good condition as well. Some vintage stores have advertised guitars with original cases, stating the condition of both the instrument **and the case!** Of course, **any** case is better than no case at all.

Another more ominous factor for pawn shops is that if a shop ever takes in a quality instrument without a case, there's a chance that the instrument might have been stolen. In 1988, I encountered a Gibson G-3 bass in a guitar store; the owner stated that it had come in without a case. A pawn shop in the same town had been broken into a year earlier, and one of the items stolen was a Gibson G-3. Serial numbers were compared; the guitar store's G-3 was as hot as a chili pepper.

Another suspicious scenario involved the discovery of an instrument that currently lists for **over $2500** in a small pawn shop located in a town of less than 5,000 people. There was no case with the instrument.

If you're a pawn shop and a cheapo guitar comes in without a case, <u>no</u> big deal; <u>but</u> please be careful however, with better quality brands. Most pawn shop owners should hopefully be able to tell if a particular instrument is a fine piece, even if they're not familiar with the brand name, so heads up if a fancy instrument doesn't have a case!

GIBSON SECONDS: From time to time, Gibson may market "irregular instruments" to the public; however, they're sold through regular retailers instead of a "factory outlet store". They're noted as seconds by either "SECOND", "SEC" or "2" being embossed on the back of the headstock, where the serial number should also be located. Gibson also stamped the designation BGN on the back of headstocks which may interpret to mean "bargain" instruments. BGN instruments are below Gibson "seconds" in quality.

Like an irregular shirt that is just as "wearable", a Gibson second is just as "playable"; the "second" designation concerns **cosmetics only**, and has nothing to do with how the instrument will play or sound. However, if two Gibson instruments of the same model from the same year **with the same amount of wear and tear on them** were compared, and one of them happened to have been marketed as a second, the "first quality" instrument would still be more valuable and desirable to most guitar buffs.

STORAGE: Any fretted instrument that is being put into storage (including instruments left for a pawn loan) should be **stored vertically, not horizontally;** that is, **cases should be stored on their sides, not flat,** which brings up the next (and obvious) point, that **cases should never be staked on top of each other!**

Another important factor regarding storage involves humidity, particularly the storage environment for instruments **during winter.** An overly dry environment will lead to all sorts of damage to instruments. There are now battery-powered humidity devices that fit inside guitar cases, but a good rule of thumb to consider might be: "If **you're** comfortable, your **guitar** will be comfortable." Keeping guitars and basses humidified during winter is an important part ot proper care.

ABOUT THE PHOTO SECTION:

First and foremost, I'm not a professional photographer ("It shows" was Malc's sardonic comment). Some years ago, I began taking photographs of interesting instruments that I encountered, simply for my own information and viewing pleasure.

However, once I began writing for <u>The National Music Trader</u> (which was to become known as <u>Vintage Guitar</u> in January of 1990), I carried my "no-frills" camera and a used sheet in my car at all times, in case I happened to stumble across something that might be worth photographing for possible placement in a future issue.

Obviously, when it was established that this book was definitely a "go", I began to snap even more photographs, many times of new instruments or used instruments that might have been relatively common at one time.

I attempted to photograph all instruments under the same conditions whenever possible, in an effort to provide some semblance of continuity. I was able to use the aforementioned sheet as a background almost all of the time (except a time or two when it had been laundered and I forgot to put it back in my car before heading out in search of more instruments). In some cases, an instrument showed up better when a flash was used, and in other cases a guitar or bass looked better without a flash (of course, in the latter situation, the wrinkles on the sheet showed up more!).

I found that photographing instruments **outside in the shade** seemed to provide the best contrast for reprinting, and I tried to photograph under these circumstances whenever possible, even if it was one of those rare occasions when I'd forgotten the sheet; any picture that didn't necessarily conform to the photo guidelines I'd established for myself was still better than no photo of a guitar or bass that I might not encounter again!

In some situations I even had to take photographs indoors (and such examples may be obvious), but it's my opinion that since this is a "budget"/"no-frills" guitar book, perhaps the photo section should be considered "no-frills" as well, particularly since the aforementioned "no-frills" 35mm camera was used. What the hell, it helps keep down the price of the book, and I did the best I could with what I had to work with... and besides, one of the books listed in the bibliography contains **almost nothing but photographs**, and the photos in this book are, in my opinion, comparable to many of the ones in that particular book.

Rather than photograph every American brand name guitar I encountered, I opted to try and get photos of many that might not have been previously seen in other guitar books, so there are quite a few of that type in this photo section. As for particular models, I didn't photograph every single Fender Stratocaster or Gibson Les Paul that I saw; I've opted here to show only a few examples of some models that may have been in production for decades, and where the year model of certain instruments are known, it shows how little certain guitars or basses might have changed over the years.

After much rumination, it was also decided that for the most part, "limited editions" and guitars or basses with other similar designations would not be shown; instruments that would have been standard production pieces during their time would be featured. Of course, many production instruments from yesteryear are now very desirable and are also rare. Some exceptions to the "production instruments only" policy will be encountered herein, however. Examples include a 1979 Fender Silver Anniversary Stratocaster and a 1982 Gibson Moderne re-issue, as both were mentioned in the text.

As for dating instruments, each piece will be dated as accurately as possible, but in many cases only a general time period will be noted, as that's as accurate as could be determined.

Where **no date** is shown with an instrument, it indicates that the guitar or bass is a **new, current production model** as of this writing, but any instrument **with a date** isn't necessarily discontinued.

Please remember that a "re-issue" may or may not be a "limited edition" instrument! For example, the 1990 Gibson Firebird re-issue shown herein is a current production model as of this writing; it is **not** a limited edition, although some other Firebird series throughout the years **have** been limited editions.

Useful information about each instrument will be found with each photo, following the name of the manufacturer, model name and year of production (or time period, as the case may be). Such information will apply only to the example shown, but may also be applicable to other examples of the same model.

Original finishes of instruments will not be noted unless the finish is a custom color or rare/discontinued type. **Modifications (including refinishing)** will be noted in parentheses, **with one exception:** Replacement tuners will not be cited, as in some cases it is difficult to ascertain whether such parts are original or aftermarket parts, and what's more, such smaller parts are probably difficult to see in these photographs. Nevertheless, please bear in mind that even if replacement tuners do a better job in the tuning department, any older instrument with such replacements will generally be worth less to a potential collector than one with its original tuners!

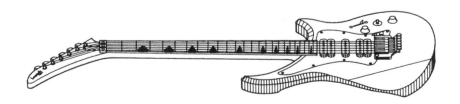

"A"

Adamas

Airline

Alembic

1 **2** **3**

4 **5** **6**

1)   1965 Aldens house brand by Harmony, a Stratotone variant - has an 'A' logo
2)   Adamas by Ovation - soundhole leaf trim made of five different woods
3)   Early Sixties Airline by Valco - 3/4 scale

4)   Sixties Airline by Kay - compare to Kay, Montclair & Truetone brand versions
5)   1982 Alembic Distillate DMSB bass - medium scale, custom-ordered features, total of six differen hardwoods including Hawaiian Flame Koa top
6)   1985 Alembic Persuader bass - medium scale, "Spoiler" body style, active electronics, zebrawood laminate on body and headstock. Alembic's lowes priced stock instrument

Ampeg

1

2

3

Baldwin

4

5

6

1) 1986 Alembic Persuader - "Vector" body style, active electronics

2) Ampeg/Dan Armstrong bass, circa 1970 - Plexiglas body, short scale

3) Ampeg/Dan Armstrong bass - Plexiglas body, short scale, rare fretless version (approximately 150 were made)

4) Baldwin by Burns Vibraslim, circa 1967 - Imported from England, controls mounted on pickguard

5) Baldwin by Burns model 706, circa 1967 - Imported from England

6) Baldwin by Burns 704 bass, circa 1967 - Imported from England

Baron

Travis Bean

Carvin

1

2

3

Catalina

Chris

4

5

6

1)   Baron tenor guitar - House brand, possibly by Jackson-Guldan, early Sixties?

2)   1976 Travis Bean Standard - Koa body, "T" logo built into headstock frame. The first production brand to feature aluminum necks on wood bodies.

3)   Carvin V-440 bass, late Eighties

4)   1987 Carvin V-220

5)   Late Sixties Catalina by Kay (logo has fallen off headstock)

6)   Chris Adjustomatic   - Sixties?

Danelectro

Dean

1) **Sixties Danelectro Bellzouki - 12-string**
2) **Mid-Sixties Danelectro - lipstick tube pickup**
3) **Sixties Danelectro model 4011**

4) **Early Sixties Danelectro Convertible - pickup is removable from soundhole to make a completely acoustic guitar!**
5) **1978 Dean Flying V**
6) **1979 Dean Elite**

Epiphone

1

2

3

4

5

6

1)   1963 Epiphone Wilshire "bat-wing" headstock made by Gibson
2)   1965 Epiphone by Gibson Olympic Double Missing two knobs)
3)   1982 Epiphone Spirit - similar to Gibson Spirit of the same year, one of the few post-1970 U.S. made Epiphones (replacement pickguard)

4)   1983 Epiphone "map" guitar - new and unsold, one of the few post-1970 U.S. made Epiphones, very rare
5)   1962 Epiphone by Gibson Century
6)   1967 Epiphone Riviera - made by Gibson, "Frequensator" tailpiece

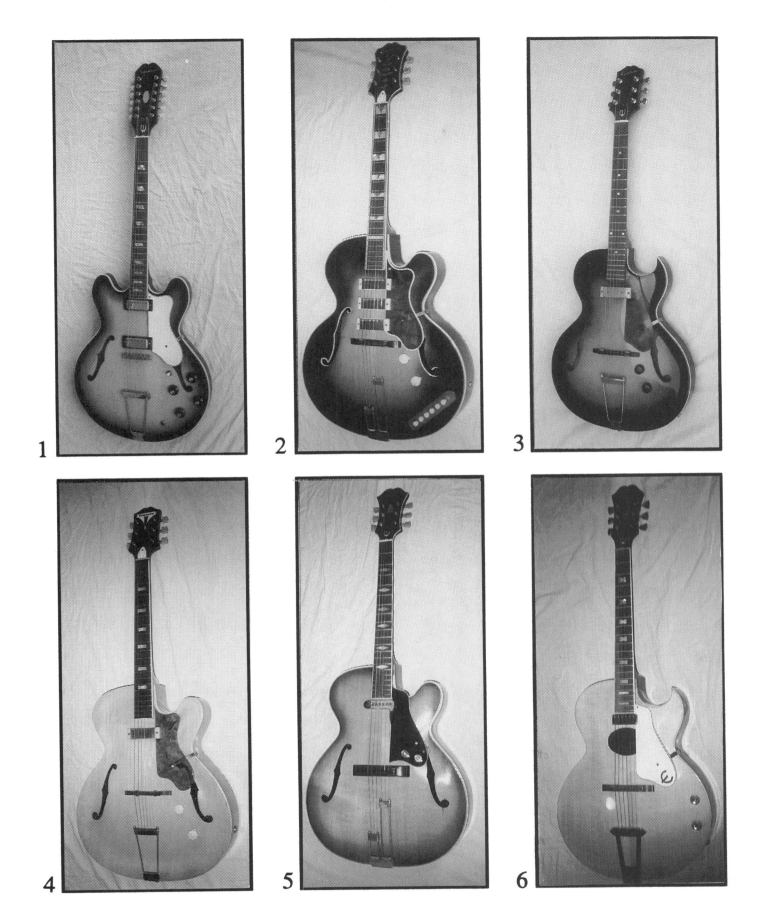

1) 1967 Epiphone by Gibson Riviera 12-string
2) 1953 Epiphone Zephyr Emperor Regent - New York-made, the "Big Daddy" of the New York Epi models
3) Epiphone Sorrento by Gibson, circa 1960
4) 1954 Epiphone Zephyr Regent - New York-made
5) 1964 Epiphone by Gibson Triumph Regent - ("floating" pickup built into replacement pickguard)
6) 1964 Epiphone by Gibson Howard Roberts

Fender

1

2

3

4

5

6

1)   1949 Epiphone FT-79 - New York made (top refinished, pickguard removed)
2)   Late Forties Epiphone Triumph - (pickguard removed, replacement tailpiece) - New York-made
3)   1964 Epiphone by Gibson FT45N Cortez

4)   1967 Epiphone by Gibson Rivoli Bass (pickguard removed)
5)   1950 Fender "No-caster"
6)   1953 Fender Telecaster

1

2

3

4

5

6

1)   1955 Fender Telecaster
2)   Mid-Sixties Fender Telecaster - (originally blond; this Tele shows how exposure to cigarette smoke can affect finish. It is now an amber color with worn spots showing the original blond)
3)   1966 Fender Telecaster

4)   1969 Fender Telecaster - Custom Color: does not match most blues found on Fender color charts; appears to be the stock blue finish that came on promotional guitars such as Mustangs
5)   1971 Fender Telecaster with vibrato
6)   1973 Fender Telecaster

1   2   3

4   5   6

1)   1973 Fender Telecaster - Custom Color: "Candy Apple Red" with matching headstock - "extremely rare"
2)   1977 Fender Telecaster
3)   1977 Fender Telecaster

4)   1983 Fender Telecaster
5)   Fender Telecaster - current
6)   1962 Fender Custom Telecaster

1)	1968 Fender Telecaster Thinline	4)	1974 Fender Telecaster Deluxe
2)	1972 Fender Telecaster Thinline - mahogany body	5)	1974 Fender Telecaster Custom
3)	1973 Fender Telecaster Thinline	6)	1983 Fender Telecaster Elite - active electronics

1

2

3

4

5

6

1) **Fender Tele Plus - current - Lace sensors**
2) **1951 Fender Esquire**
3) **1956 Fender Stratocaster - "pre CBS"**

4) **1959 Fender Stratocaster -"pre-CBS"**
5) **1961 Fender Stratocaster -"pre-CBS"**
6) **1963 Fender Stratocaster - non-pearl/ "clay dot" fret markers**

1

2

3

4

5

6

1) **1964 Fender Stratocaster** -"pre CBS", non-pearl/"clay dot" markers, excellent/near-mint condition

2) **Sixties Fender Stratocaster** - Custom Color: Lake Placid Blue

3) **1974 Fender Stratocaster** - (autographed by Jeff Beck, Robin Tower and the late Stevie Ray Vaughan)

4) **Mid Seventies Fender Stratocaster** "hardtail"/no vibrato

5) **1979 Fender Silver Anniversary Limited Edition Stratocaster** -Silver Porsche automobile paint!

6) **1982 Fender Stratocaster**

77

1) 1983 Fender Stratocaster - short-lived version with only two knobs and right-angle jack

2) 1983 Fender Stratocaster - short-lived version with only two knobs and right-angle jack

3) 1989 Fender Stratocaster American Standard - short-lived "Graffiti Yellow" finish

4) Fender Stratocaster - American Standard - current

5) Fender "U.S. Vintage '62" Stratocaster - re-issue - current

6) 1980 Fender "The Strat" - upgrade wiring, bridge & knobs gold-plate hardware, matching headstock

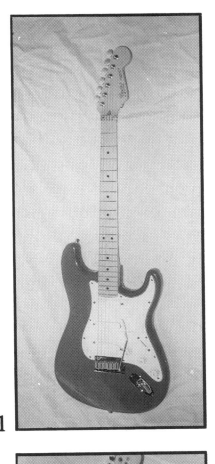

1

2

3

4

5

6

1) Fender Strat Plus - current, Lace sensors
2) Fender Strat Plus - current, Lace sensors
3) 1988 Fender Stratocaster - "Eric Clapton Signature" model

4) 1970 Fender Jazzmaster
5) 1964 Fender Jaguar -
"clay dot"/non-pearl fret markers "pre-CBS"
6) 1965 Fender Jaguar - (originally Ice Blue, has turned a greenish color due to exposure to cigarette smoke) - note hang tag

1) 1966 Fender Jaguar
2) 1968 Fender Jaguar - Custom Color:
"Candy Apple Red"
3) 1970 Fender Jaguar

4) 1957 Fender Musicmaster - "pre-CBS"
5) 1961 Fender Musicmaster - "pre-CBS"
6) 1966 Fender Musicmaster

1)   **Late-Sixties Fender Musicmaster**
2)   **1971 Fender Musicmaster - (yellowed due to exposure to cigarette smoke, dragon decal added)**
3)   **1963 Fender Duo-Sonic - "pre-CBS"**

4)   **1963 Fender Duo-Sonic - "pre-CBS"**
5)   **1965 Fender Duo-Sonic II (replacement bridge)**
6)   **1965 Fender Mustang**

1) 1966 Fender Mustang
2) 1967 Fender Mustang - "Competition" version in "Lake Placid Blue" with racing stripe and matching headstock (missing pickup covers)
3) 1969 Fender Mustang - "Competition" version with matching headstock and racing stripe

4) 1966 Fender Electric XII
5) 1969 Fender Swinger/Musiclander "Arrow" guitar - "rare"
6) 1967 Fender Coronado XII 12-string

1)   1971 Fender Bronco
2)   1982 Fender Lead II
3)   Fender King flat-top, circa 1967 - apparently a
type of Fender flat-top that was not marketed
extensively; "very rare"

4)   Late Sixties Fender Villager 12-string
5)   1969 Fender by Harmony
6)   Sixties Fender by Harmony - tortoise-shell
headstock trim that matches pickguard - hubba hubba!

1) 1958 Fender Precision bass - (pickup cover and bridge/tailpiece cover removed) -"pre-CBS"
2) 1958 Fender Precision bass - "pre-CBS"
3) 1966 Fender Precision bass - (pickup cover removed)
4) 1973 Fender Precision bass
5) 1974 Fender Precision bass
6) 1975 Fender Precision bass - (pickup cover removed)

1) Late-Seventies Fender Precision bass - "Antigua" finish
2) Late-Seventies Fender Precision bass - relatively rare maple fretless version (bridge/tailpiece cover removed)
3) Fender "'57 Precision" Vintage Re-issue - current
4) 1980 Fender Precision Special bass - matching headstock, gold hardware and active electronics
5) Early-Eighties Fender Precision Elite - two pickups, active electronics
6) Fender Precision Plus bass - current - two Lace Sensors

1)   1966 Fender Jazz Bass - (pickup covers removed)
2)   1966 Fender Jazz Bass - Custom Color: Candy
Apple Red (pickup covers removed)
3)   1973 Fender Jazz Bass - short-lived maple
neck/fretboard with black block markers and black
binding, Custom Color: Telecaster Blond"

4)   Mid-Seventies Fender Jazz Bass
5)   Fender Jazz Bass - current -
note longer upper body horn
6)   Body of late-Sixties Fender Telecaster Bass
(first style) in Paisley finish (missing knobs)

1) 1972 Fender Telecaster Bass - (bridge cover reversed!)
2) 1966 Fender Mustang Bass
3) 1970 Fender Mustang Bass - "Competition" version with racing stripe
4) Fender Mustang Bass - early-Seventies, left-handed, relatively rare sunburst finish
5) 1976 Fender Mustang Bass
6) 1971 Fender Musicmaster Bass

1

2

Five Star

3

Fritz Bros.

4

5

6

1) Late-Seventies Fender Musicmaster Bass - rare translucent red finish
2) 1967 Fender Coronado I bass
3) 1966 Fender Coronado Bass II

4) Fender JP-90 Bass - current
5) 1960 Five Star by Harmony - a Stella-variant house brand - has five star-shaped markers
6) Fritz Bros. "Roy Buchanan Deluxe" - rare version with Buchanan's name on headstock

G & L

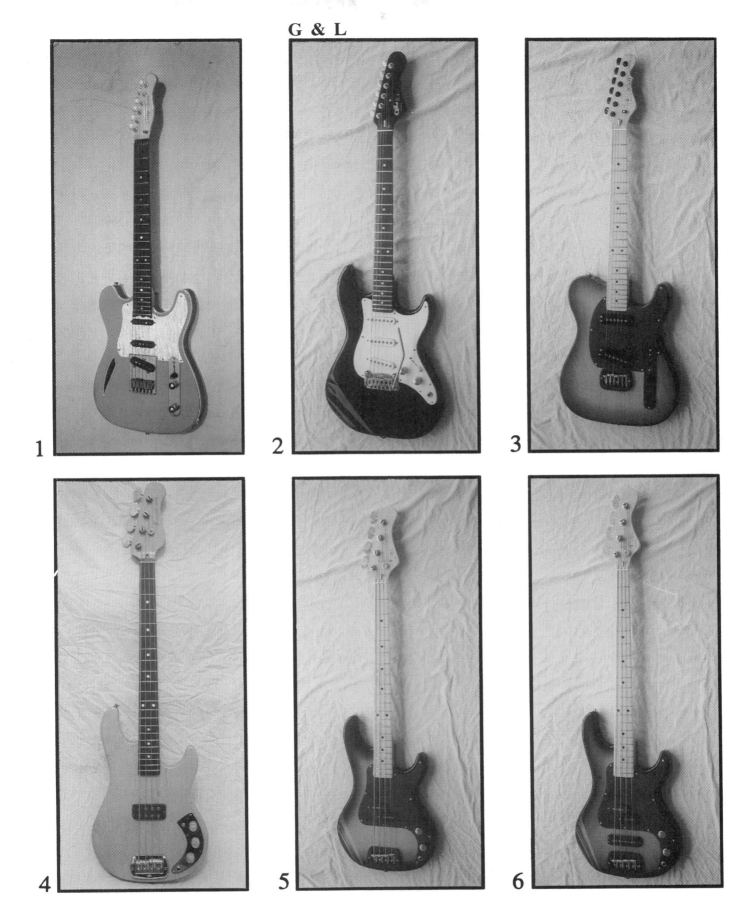

1)   Fritz Bros. Deluxe
2)   G & L SC-3
3)   G & L ASAT
4)   Early-Eighties G & L L-1000 bass
5)   G & L SB-2 bass
6)   G & L SB-1 bass

Gibson

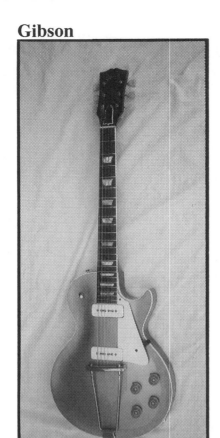

1

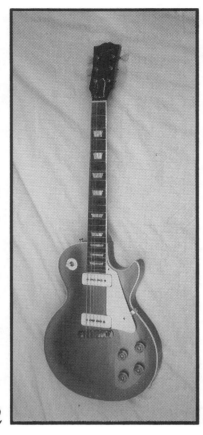

2

3

4

5

6

1)   1952 Gibson Les Paul - first year production
2)   1953 Gibson Les Paul
3)   1958 Gibson Les Paul Standard

4)   1959 Gibson Les Paul Standard
5)   Early Sixties Gibson SG/Les Paul Standard
6)   Early Sixties Gibson SG/Les Paul Standard - rare ebony tailblock

1

2

3

4

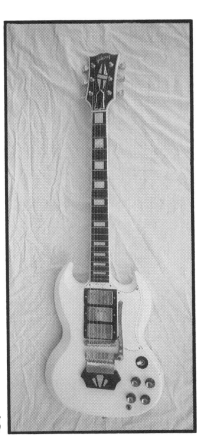

5

6

1)   1978 Gibson Les Paul Standard
2)   1989 Gibson Les Paul Standard
3)   1989 Gibson Les Paul Standard
"Gold-top re-issue"

4)   1990 Gibson "1960 Classic" Les Paul
Standard re-issue
5)   Early Sixties Gibson SG/Les Paul Custom -
Rare ebony tailblock
6)   Early Seventies Gibson Les Paul Custom -
(replacement pickups)

91

1

2

3

4

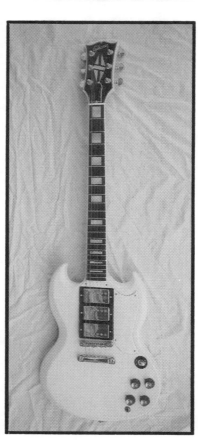

5

6

1)   1977 Gibson Les Paul Custom - "Silverburst" finish

2)   1979 Gibson Les Paul Custom

3)   1979 Gibson Les Paul Custom - lefty

4)   1980 Gibson Les Paul Custom - (replacement treble pickup)

5)   1989 Gibson SG/Les Paul Custom re-issue

6)   1958 Gibson Les Paul Jr. - 3/4 scale version

1

2

3

4

5

6

1)	1959 Gibson Les Paul Jr.	4)	1960 Gibson Les Paul Special "TV" finish
2)	1986 Gibson Les Paul Jr. re-issue	5)	1990 Gibson Les Paul Special re-issue
3)	1989 Gibson Les Paul Jr. re-issue	6)	1971 Gibson Les Paul Deluxe

1

2

3

4

5

6

1) 1974 Gibson Les Paul Deluxe - rare red sparkle/metalflake top (replacement pickups, pickguard removed)
2) 1975 Gibson Les Paul Deluxe
3) 1976 Gibson Les Paul Recording (missing pickguard)

4) Mid-Seventies Gibson Les Paul Signature
5) 1978 Gibson "The Paul"
6) 1980 Gibson L.P. Firebrand

1

2

3

4

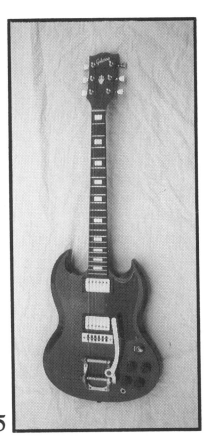

5

6

1) 1985 Gibson Les Paul LP-XPL
2) 1989 Gibson Les Paul Studio - dot markers, no binding
3) 1966 Gibson SG Standard (vibrato mechanism removed)

4) 1969 Gibson SG Standard
5) 1972 Gibson SG Standard
6) 1974 Gibson SG Standard

1

2

3

4

5

6

1)   1973 Gibson SG Standard
2)   1988 Gibson SG
3)   1990 Gibson SG -
  "TV Yellow" finish

4)   1978 Gibson SG Custom
5)   1965 Gibson SG Jr. -
  (replacement truss rod cover)
6)   1963 Gibson SG Special

1

2

3

4

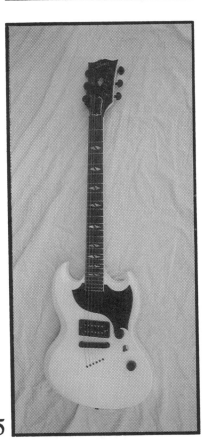

5

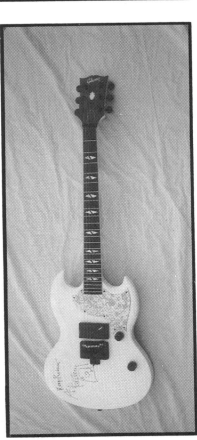

6

1) **1971 Gibson SG-200**
2) **1971 Gibson SG-250**
3) **1979 Gibson "The SG"**

4) **1980 Gibson SG Firebrand**
5) **1987 Gibson SG '90 Double**
6) **1988 Gibson SG '90 -**
(autographed by Ace Frehley)

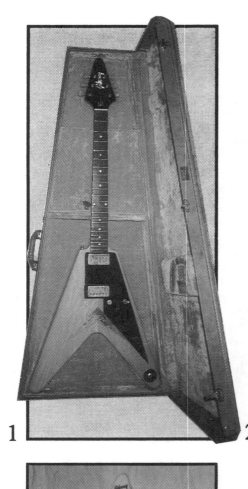

1

2

3

4

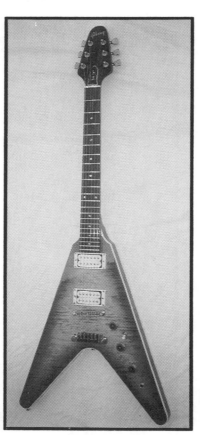

5

6

1) 1958 Gibson Flying V - shown in original plush-lined case
2) 1979 Gibson Flying V
3) 1984 Gibson Flying V Korina re-issue - relatively rare black finish

4) 1984 Gibson Flying V - factory graphics (yellowed due to cigarette smoke, original finish was white)
5) 1984 Gibson "The V" - bound maple top
6) 1987 Gibson V-90

1) **Gibson Flying V - current**
2) **Gibson Flying V - current**
3) **1976 Gibson Explorer re-issue**

4) **1982 Gibson "E2" Explorer -**
bound maple top, gold hardware
5) **1983 Gibson Explorer E2 - bound top**
6) **1984 Gibson Explorer - Gibson vibrato**

1

2

3

4

5

6

1) 1984 Gibson Explorer - factory graphics
2) Gibson Explorer - current
3) Gibson Explorer - current
4) 1960 Gibson Melody Maker
5) 1960 Gibson Melody Maker - (refinished, replacement bridge/tailpiece)
6) 1962 Gibson Melody Maker

1

2

3

4

5

6

1) 1965 Gibson Melody Maker
2) 1967 Gibson Melody Maker
3) 1977 Gibson Melody Maker re-issue - this body
style is the shape of the first double-cutaway Melody
Makers that appeared in the early Sixties

4) 1987 Gibson Melody Maker
5) 1963 Gibson Firebird 3
6) 1963 Gibson Firebird I

1) 1963 Gibson Firebird I with vibrato
2) 1982 Gibson Firebird II - bound maple top, full-size humbuckers, active electronics, "extremely rare"
3) 1990 Gibson Firebird re-issue

4) 1974 Gibson L-6S Custom - set-in neck, Natural finish version with maple fretboard
5) 1975 Gibson L-6S Custom - set-in neck, Black version with ebony fretboard
6) 1977 Gibson L-6S Deluxe - simpler controls than L-6S Custom, strings load through the body, rare version with set-in neck; most L-6S Deluxes seen by author had bolt-on necks

1

2

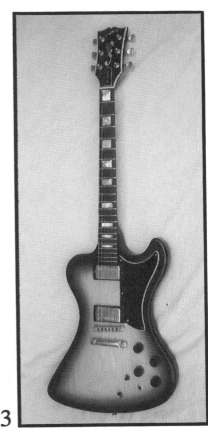

3

4

5

6

1) 1975 Gibson L-6 Deluxe
2) 1975 Gibson Marauder
3) 1978 Gibson RD Artist - active electronics

4) 1977 Gibson RD Artist - active electronics
5) 1977 Gibson RD Standard
6) 1978 Gibson RD Standard

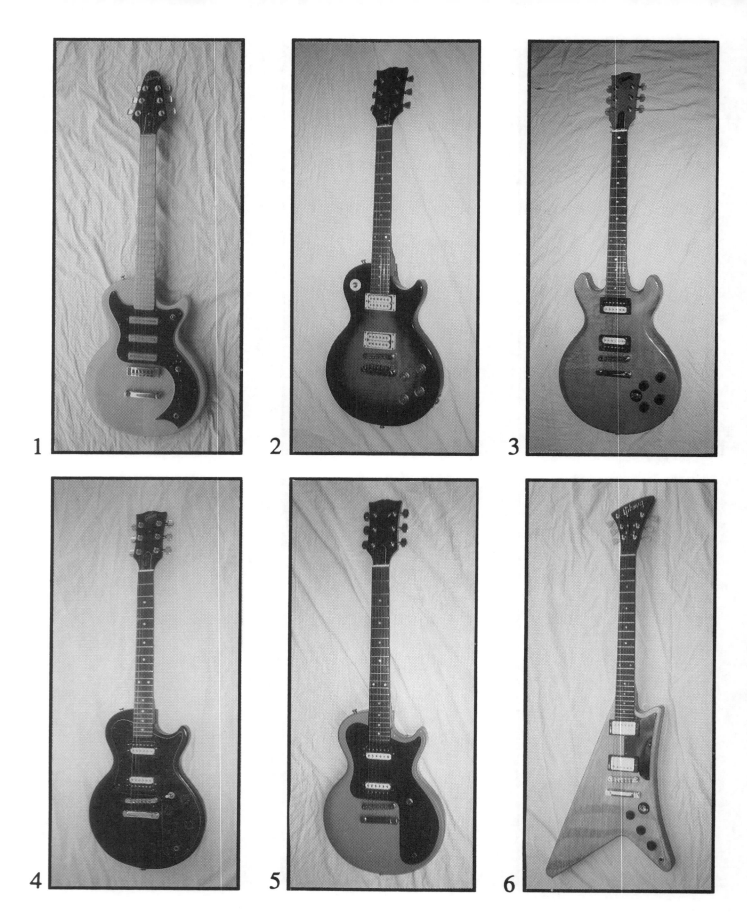

1) 1977 Gibson S-1
2) 1979 Gibson GK-55 - the model number is a reference to a specific Gibson sales territory; this was marketed in that territory only
3) 1980 Gibson Firebrand ES-335S

4) 1981 Gibson Sonex 180 - composite body
5) 1981 Gibson Sonex 180 - composite body
6) 1982 Gibson Moderne re-issue

104

1

2

3

4

5

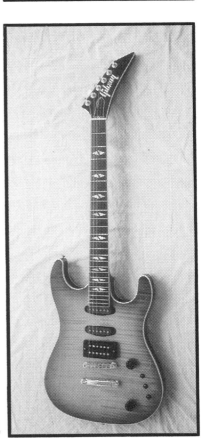

6

1) 1984 Gibson Moderne re-issue
2) 1983 Gibson Futura
3) 1983 Gibson Corvus I
4) 1983 Gibson Challenger - bolt-on neck
5) 1984 Gibson Invader
6) 1987 Gibson US-1 - Cherry Sunburst finish

1

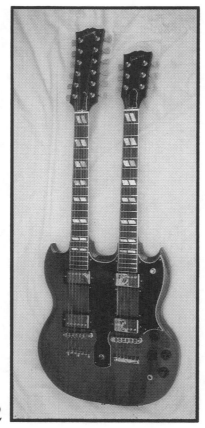

2

3

4

5

6

1) 1987 Gibson US-1 - Natural finish
2) 1988 Gibson EDS-1275
3) 1961 Gibson ES-335TD

4) 1963 Gibson ES-335TDC
5) 1972 Gibson ES-335TD
6) 1981 Gibson ES-335TD - short-lived version
with coil tap switch on lower cutaway

1)   1983 Gibson ES-335 DOT re-issue
2)   1987 Gibson ES-335TD
3)   Gibson ES-335 - current

4)   1989 Gibson ES-335 Studio - no f-holes, no binding on neck
5)   1959 Gibson ES-345TD
6)   1964 Gibson ES-330TDC - chrome P-90 pickups (pickguard removed)

1) 1965 Gibson ES-330TDC
2) 1971 Gibson ES-320TDN - rarest of all thinlines (bridge/tailpiece cover removed)
3) 1974 Gibson ES-325TD

4) Gibson Trini Lopez - circa 1968
5) 1989 Gibson B.B. King Lucille - no f-holes
6) Gibson ES-125, circa 1950

1

2

3

4

5

6

1)   1956 Gibson ES-125
2)   1957 Gibson ES-125T 3/4
3)   1960 Gibson ES-125T

4)   1966 Gibson ES-125CD (missing pickguard)
5)   1967 Gibson ES-125TDC
6)   1957 Gibson ES-225T

1

2

3

4

5

6

1) 1958 Gibson ES-225TD
2) 1958 Gibson ES-175 (pickguard removed)
3) 1953 Gibson ES-175D

4) 1953 Gibson ES-175D (missing pickguard)
5) 1964 Gibson ES-175D (replacement bridge)
6) 1953 Gibson ES-295

1

2

3

4

5

6

1) 1961 Gibson Tal Farlow - "very rare: look at the flame maple top on this one!!!"
2) Early Seventies Gibson L-5CES (replacement volume knob)
3) 1978 Gibson ES-350T

4) 1965 Gibson ES-120T
5) Gibson L-3, circa 1915 (pickguard removed, replacement bridge and tailpiece)
6) Gibson L-0, circa 1928

1) Gibson L-0, circa 1929 -
additional fret markers
2) Thirties, Gibson L-0
3) 1938 Gibson L-10

4) 1947 Gibson L-7
5) 1957 Gibson L-48
6) Fifties Gibson L-48 -
(pickguard modified)

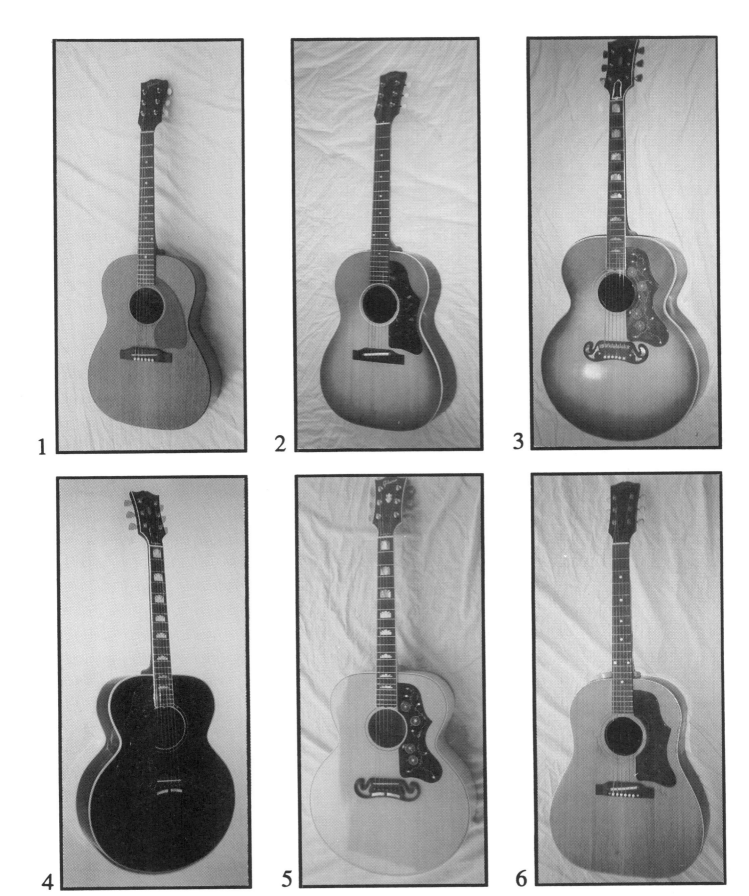

1)	Early Sixties Gibson LGO	4)	Gibson J-200 - current, left-handed
2)	1961 Gibson B-25	5)	Gibson J-200 - current
3)	1965 Gibson J-200	6)	Gibson J-50, circa 1965

1) 1966 Gibson J-50
2) Early Seventies Gibson B-25
3) Gibson B-25-12, circa 1968

4) Late Sixties Gibson B-15 - one of the most promotional Gibson guitars ever made; note the narrow, Melody Maker-like headstock
5) 1964 Gibson Hummingbird
6) 1970 Gibson Hummingbird - Natural-finish top

1)   **1979 Gibson Hummingbird - block markers instead of double parellelogram**
2)   **Early Seventies Gibson Dove Custom - Cherry Sunburst finish**
3)   **Early Seventies Gibson Gospel**

4)   **1969 Gibson EB-1 bass re-issue - short scale**
5)   **1968 Gibson EB-2 bass - baritone switch, short scale (pickguard removed)**
6)   **Early Seventies Gibson EB-2D bass**

1

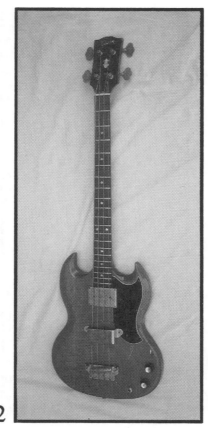

2

3

4

5

6

1)   1965 Gibson EB-0 bass - plain bridge/tailpiece with mute, short scale
2)   1965 Gibson EB-0 bass - plain bridge/tailpiece, handrest, short scale
3)   1968 Gibson EB-0 bass - short scale, improved bridge/tailpiece assembly (bridge/tailpiece cover removed, professionally refinished)

4)   1973 Gibson EB-0 bass
5)   1970 Gibson EB-3 bass - short scale, short-lived version with slotted headstock and rear-projecting/"banjo" tuners
6)   1973 Gibson EB-3 bass - short scale (bridge/tailpiece cover removed)

1

2

3

4

5

6

1) 1969 Gibson Les Paul Professional bass (tailpiece cover removed)
2) 1976 Gibson Thunderbird bass - Bicentennial Limited Edition
3) 1974 Gibson Ripper bass

4) 1976 Gibson Ripper bass - fretless
5) 1975 Gibson G-3 bass
6) 1975 Gibson Grabber bass - sliding pickup

Gower

1) 1980 Gibson RD Artist bass
2) 1981 Gibson RD-CMT Artist bass - bound, flame maple top, "Antique Sunburst" finish, "very rare"
3) 1981 Gibson Victory Standard bass - new and unsold

4) 1984 Gibson Explorer bass
5) 1987 Gibson IV bass
6) Mid-Sixties Gower G-55-2

Gretsch

1

2

3

4

5

6

1)   1954 Gretsch Duo-Jet 6128 - older "script" logo
2)   Late fifties Gretsch Duo-Jet 6128 - modern "T-roof" logo
3)   1955 Gretsch Country Club 6103 - "Cadillac Green" finish

4)   Fifties Gretsch Country Club 6192
5)   1957 Gretsch Jet Firebird 6131
6)   1963 Gretsch Corvette 6132 - "3 + 3" headstock

1)   1966 Gretsch Corvette 6135 - "2 + 4" headstock, vibrato (refinished, missing knobs)
2)   1964 Gretsch Nashville 6120
3)   1965 Gretsch Tennessean 6119

4)   1966 Gretsch Tennessean 6119
5)   1967 Gretsch Tennessean 6119
6)   1963 Gretsch Chet Atkins Tennessean 6119

1

2

3

4

5

6

1) 1956 Gretsch Chet Atkins solidbody 6121 - Western scenes carved on fret markers, leather-bound sides and a real 'G' brand on top. Yee-hah!
2) 1962 Gretsch Chet Atkins model 6120
3) 1973 Gretsch Country Gentleman 7670

4) 1967 Gretsch Country Gentleman 6122
5) 1974 Gretsch Country Gentleman 7670
6) 1962 Gretsch Sal Salvador 6199

1)   1963 Gretsch Single Anniversary
2)   1967 Gretsch 12-string Electric 6075
3)   1967 Gretsch Rally 6105 - (controls re-arranged, replacement pickguard)
4)   1967 Gretsch White Falcon 7595
5)   1967 Gretsch Monkees
6)   1968 Gretsch Viking 6187

Guild

1   2   3

4   5   6

1) **1968 Gretsch George Van Eps 6079 - 7-string version with lower bass string (missing bridge & tailpiece)**
2) **Sixties Gretsch budget flat-top**
3) **1976 Gretsch Sun Valley 7515**

4) **1957 Guild CE-100**
5) **1961 Guild T-50**
6) **1966 Guild Duane Eddy 400**

1) **Mid-Eighties Guild D-40**
2) **Mid-Eighties Guild D-25NT - lefty**
3) **1971 Guild F-40**

4) **1972 Guild ST-302-SB**
5) **1973 Guild S-100 - "upgrade"**
version with oak leaf and acorn body routing, natural finish and clear pickguard
6) **1977 Guild S-300 (missing volume knob)**

1

2

Hamer

3

4

5

6

1)   1974 Guild M-85 bass -
new & unsold - note hang tags
2)   1977 Guild B-301 bass
3)   1978 Guild B302-A bass

4)   Mid-Eighties Guild F45-CE
5)   1980 Hamer Special
6)   1987 Hamer Scarab

125

1) Hamer "Steve Stevens" model
2) Mid-Eighties Hamer Prototype
3) Mid-Eighties Hamer Phantom
4) 1987 Hamer Blitz - factory graphics
5) Late Eighties Hamer Vector - factory graphics
6) 1983 Hamer Blitz bass

Heritage   # Harmony

1

2

3

4

5

6

1) 1988 Heritage H-140CM
2) 1989 Heritage H-535
3) Early Sixties Harmony Stratotone
H47 "Mercury" variant

4) Early Sixties Harmony Rocket - relatively unusual
version with three pickups and single cutaway
5) 1970 Harmony Rocket
6) Mid-Sixties Harmony H-77 - three pickups with
separate off/on switches, tortoise-shell headstock

1) Harmony Meteor, circa 1964
2) 1969 Harmony thinline - compare to Silvertone
3) Mid-Sixties Harmony H-79 12-string
4) Fifties Harmony Master
5) Fifties Harmony Monterey
6) 1970 Harmony Sovereign

Holiday

1

2

3

Jackson

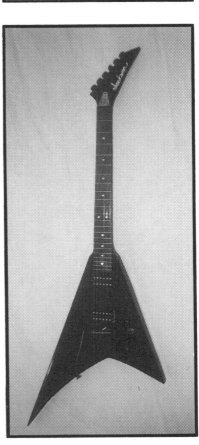

4

5

6

1) Sixties Harmony 12-string
2) 1964 Harmony H22 bass - short scale
3) Sixties Harmony bass - short scale, has rocker switches for 2 pickups, but only has one pickup---?

4) Early Sixties Holiday by Harmony house brand, Stratotone variant
5) Jackson Soloist - Factory graphics
6) 1981 Jackson "Randy Rhoads" model

Kalamazoo

Kay

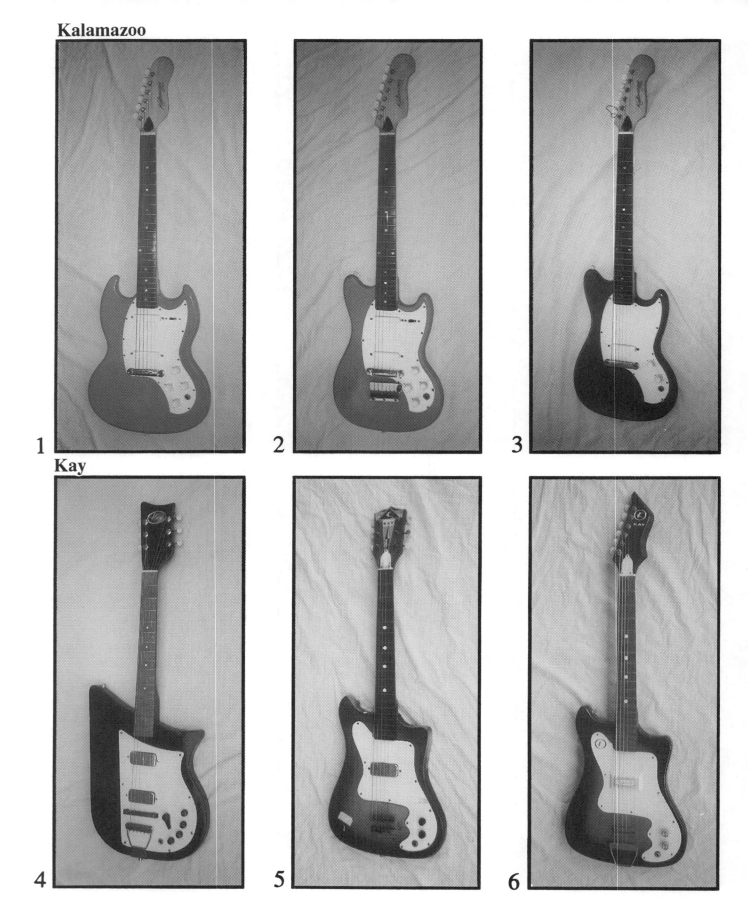

1) **Mid-Sixties Kalamazoo by Gibson -** "SG" body style
2) **Mid-Sixties Kalamazoo by Gibson -** "Fender-ish" body style (missing vibrato arm)
3) **Sixties Kalamazoo by Gibson**

4) **Late Fifties Kay "pallet guitar"**
5) **1965 Kay**
6) **Mid-Sixties Kay -** "bush axe" headstock, pickup concealed under 'hump' on pickguard! - trapeze tailpiece

1

2

3

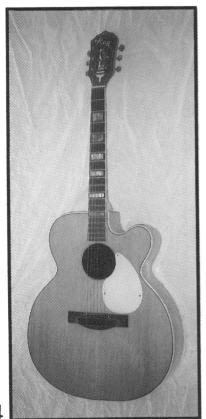

4

5

6

1)   Late Sixties Kay - bush axe headstock
2)   1966 Kay thinline - bush axe headstock
3)   Late Sixties Kay - appears to have
imported pickups

4)   Fifties Kay flat-top
5)   Fifties Kay arch-top
6)   Sixties Kay flat-top
(logo has fallen off headstock)

Old Kraftsman

Kramer

1) **Sixties Kay flat-top**
2) **Fifties Kay bass**
3) **Old Kraftsman - Fifties or Sixties - probably made by Harmony or Kay**

4) **Sixties Old Kraftsman by Kay**
5) **1979 Kramer 450 Deluxe - "tuning fork" headstock, aluminum neck**
6) **1982 Kramer Pacer Deluxe**

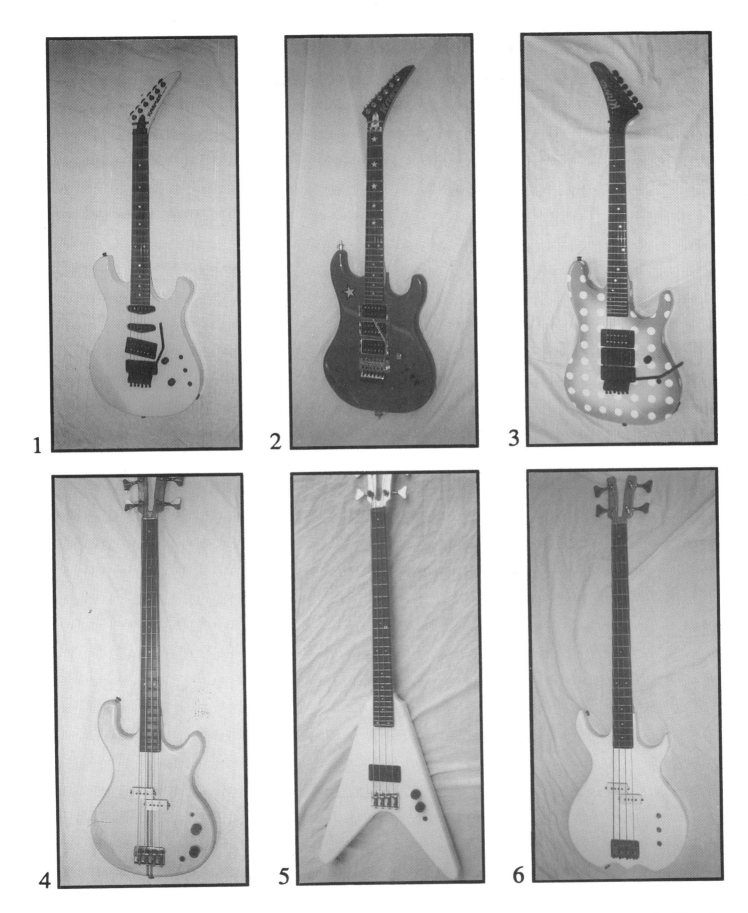

1) 1986 Kramer "Paul Dean Signature" model - relatively rare
2) 1986 Kramer Richie Sambora Signature - factory graphics
3) 1990 Kramer Nightswan

4) 1979 Kramer 4001 bass - aluminum neck, Ebonol fretboard, tuning fork headstock, rarer than the 4000 (which has active electronics)
5) 1982 Kramer Vanguard Standard bass - aluminum neck, Ebonol fretboard, tuning fork headstock, short scale
6) 1983 Kramer Stagemaster Standard bass (missing knobs) - aluminum neck, Ebonol fretboard, tuning fork headstock

Kubicki

Kustom

Martin

1   2   3

4   5   6

1) 1983 Kramer Duke Deluxe - "Deluxe" features meant a Schaller bridge and Schaller "Double J" pickup; last of the aluminum neck Kramers, short scale

2) Phillip Kubicki X-Factor bass - medium scale, flip lever de-tunes lowest string by two notes

3) Late Sixties Kustom K-200

4) 1938 C.F. Martin R-18
5) 1961 C.F. Martin 0-18
6) 1953 C.F. Martin 000-18

1) 1957 C.F. Martin 000-18
2) 1973 C.F. Martin D-18
3) 1971 C.F. Martin D-28
4) 1988 C.F. Martin D-35D
5) 1973 C.F. Martin D-35
6) 1968 C.F. Martin D-45
(replacement pickguard)

Micro-Frets

1) 1988 C.F. Martin D-42 -
#62 of a total of 75 made
2) 1976 C.F. Martin D-76 -
star-shaped fret markers, eagle logo
1,976 were made for the Bicentennial
3) 1980 C.F. Martin D-19M

4) 1980 C.F. Martin EM-18 -
1375 were made
5) Micro-Frets Stage II, circa 1971
6) Seventies Micro-Frets bass

Montclair   Mosrite

1)   **1965 Montclair by Kay**
2)   **1964 Mosrite "Ventures II" model**
3)   **1965 Mosrite "Ventures Model" bass - short scale**
4)   **1971 Mosrite**
5)   **1971 Mosrite Celebrity III**
6)   **1976 Mosrite "Brass Rail" - exposed brass rod in center of fretboard to help increase sustain**

Music Man

1

National

2

Ovation

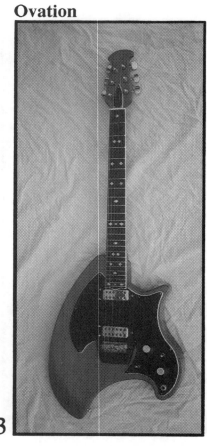

3

4

5

6

1) 1980 Music Man Sabre I
2) Late Sixties National "Bobbie Thomas" signature model - "bat" f-holes
3) Seventies Ovation Deacon

4) 1979 Ovation UK II
5) Seventies Ovation Preacher Deluxe
6) 1982 Ovation 1617

Peavey

1) Ovation Custom Legend 1767
2) Ovation "Banner Thomas" bass -
single-pickup instrument based on Magnum
series, late Seventies possibly a one-off.
3) Early Eighties Peavey T-60

4) Mid-Eighties Peavey T-15
5) Mid-Eighties Peavey T-30
6) Early Eighties Peavey Mystic

1) Early Eighties Peavey Razer
2) Peavey Falcon - current
3) Peavey Generation S-1 - current
4) Early Eighties Peavey T-40
5) Peavey Dyna-Bass, active electronics
6) Peavey Foundation bass

Penncrest **Premier**

Redondo **Rex** **B.C. Rich**

1) Peavey Fury bass
2) Fifties Penncrest by Kay
3) Mid-Sixties Premier Bantam -
probably assembled domestically
from imported parts

4) Redondo by Harmony - Sixties
5) Rex - by Kay? - Fifties?
6) 1981 B.C. Rich Mockingbird

Rickenbacker

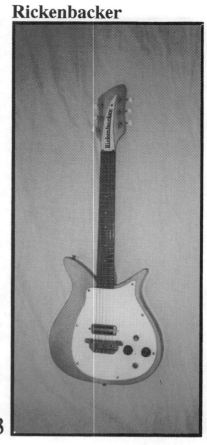

1

2

3

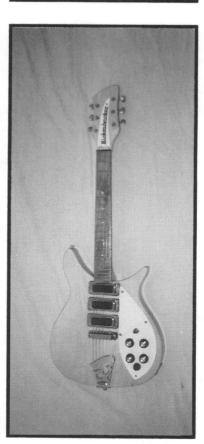

4

5

6

1)   1988 B.C. Rich TC-3
2)   1980 B.C. Rich Eagle bass
3)   1963 Rickenbacker 900 -
short scale, "tulip" body shape
(modified body)

4)   1981 Rickenbacker 320 - short scale
5)   1982 Rickenbacker 320 - short scale
6)   1968 Rickenbacker 340

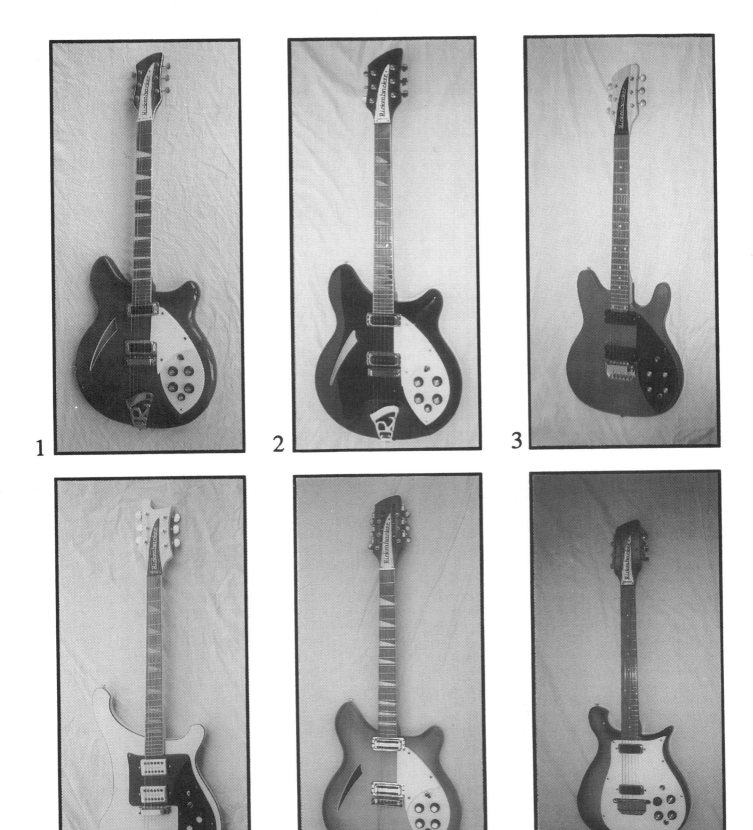

1)   1971 Rickenbacker 360 - bound headstock, slanted frets
2)   Rickenbacker 360 - current
3)   1975 Rickenbacker model 430 - bolt-on neck, new & unsold
4)   1976 Rickenbacker 481 - slanted frets
5)   1966 Rickenbacker 360-12 - 12-string
6)   1981 Rickenbacker 450-12 - 12-string

1

2

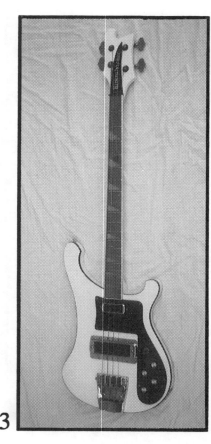

3

4

5

6

1)   1972 Rickenbacker 4001 Stereo bass -
"checkered" binding, "crushed pearl" fret markers,
"chrome bar" bass pickup
2)   1973 Rickenbacker 4001 Stereo bass
3)   1975 Rickenbacker 4001 Stereo bass -
(rear pickup cover removed, slightly yellowed due to
exposure to cigarette smoke; originally white)

4)   1975 Rickenbacker 4001 Stereo bass -
discontinued Burgundyglo finish (rear pickup cover
removed)
5)   1978 Rickenbacker 4001 Stereo bass
6)   1979 Rickenbacker 4001 Stereo bass

Roy Rogers

Robin

1)   1984 Rickenbacker 4001/V63 Vintage Series bass
2)   1980 Rickenbacker 4002 bass - rarest and fanciest of the Rickenbacker solidbody production basses
3)   1986 Rickenbacker 4003 Stereo bass - different truss rod system from 4001 model

4)   1988 Rickenbacker 4003 Stereo bass
5)   1957 Roy Rogers by Harmony - a Stella variant
6)   Robin Raider - late Eighties

145

Schecter

Silvertone

1) Robin Ranger bass - medium (32") scale, late eighties

2) Schecter Strat-style - (the mirrored pickguard may or may not be original)

3) Schecter "Tele style", circa 1984

4) Fifties Silvertone by Danelectro (pickguard removed)

5) Silvertone by Danelectro, circa 1960 "coke bottle" headstock

6) Silvertone by Danelectro, Sixties - lipstick tube pickups, concentric volume & tone controls

1) **1962 Silvertone by Danelectro**
2) **Silvertone by Harmony, circa 1960 - a Stratotone variant**
3) **Mid-Sixties Silvertone by Harmony**
4) **Sixties Silvertone by Harmony**
5) **Mid-Sixties Silvertone by Harmony**
6) **Mid-Sixties Silvertone by Kay**

1

2

3

4

5

6

1) Fifties Silvertone by Harmony
2) Fifties Silvertone by Harmony - aluminum binding! (pickguard removed)
3) Fifties Silvertone by Kay arch top (replacement treble pickup)

4) Sixties Silvertone by Harmony - compare to Harmony version
5) Early fifties Silvertone by Harmony - a Stella variant
6) Early Fifties Silvertone by Harmony - arch-top

Paul Reed Smith

1)   Sixties Silvertone by Harmony
2)   Sixties Silvertone by Harmony
3) Silvertone by Harmony- a Stella variant, circa who knows and who cares. . .

4)   1969 Silvertone by Harmony - 12-string compare to the Harmony version
5)   Early Sixties Silvertone by Danelectro bass: "dolphin nose" head-stock
6)   1985 Paul Reed Smith Custom - rare Teal color

Steinberger

1) 1987 Paul Reed Smith Custom -
"10 Grade" flame maple top, "bird" fret inlays
2) 1987 Paul Reed Smith Custom -
"bird" fret markers
3) 1988 Paul Reed Smith Custom

4) 1988 Paul Reed Smith Standard
5) Paul Reed Smith Special - bolt-on
neck - current
6) Steinberger GL4T -
all-composite construction

1

2

Stella

3

4

5

6

1) **Steinberger GR-4 - composite neck, maple body**

2) **Steinberger XP-2T4 bass - composite neck, maple body - vibrato**

3) **Steinberger SM-3 bass - composite neck, maple body**

4) **Steinberger Q-4 bass - composite neck, maple body**

5) **Stella by Harmony - circa who knows and who cares...**

6) **Stella by Harmony tenor guitar - circa who knows and who cares...**

151

Spector   **Supro**

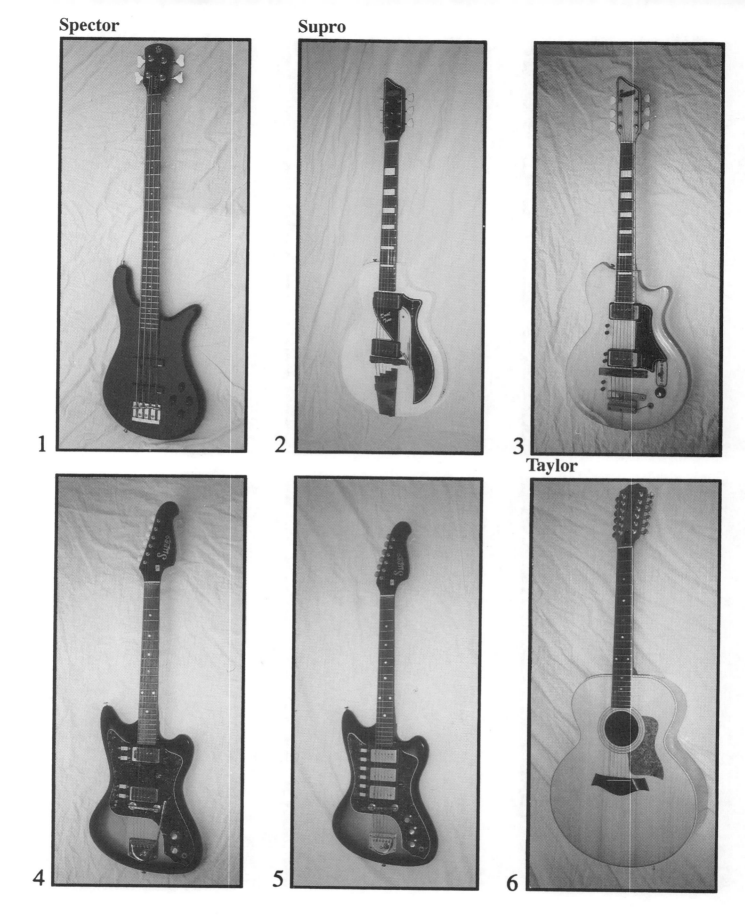

Taylor

1   2   3

4   5   6

1) **1990 Spector NST bass - active electronics**
2) **Supro Dual Tone, circa 1960**
3) **Early Sixties Supro Martinique -**
 third pickup built into bridge

4) **Mid-Sixties Supro Clermont**
5) **Late Sixties Supro Stratford**
6) **Taylor model 655 - 12-string**

Truetone

1

2

3

Valco

4

5

Washburn

6

1)   Mid-Sixties Truetone by Kay
2)   Truetone by Kay, circa 1960 (pickguard removed)
3)   Truetone by Kay arch-top electric, circa 1965 (missing pickguard)

4)   Valco-made 3/4 scale bass - finger-rest and thumb-rest, second pickup built into bridge (brand name has fallen off headstock, missing knob)
5)   1965 Valco-made bass - finger-rest and thumb-rest, second pickup inside bridge, (unknown house brand, label has fallen off headstock)
6)   Washburn Presentation, circa 1900

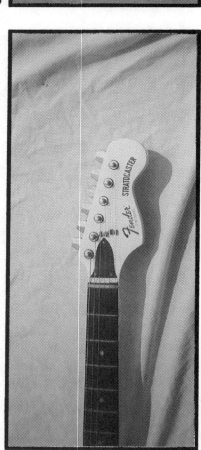

1)   Counterfeit "Fender Jazz" bass (add-on graphics, replacement tuner) -has wrong type of bridge/tailpiece cover, cheap pickups, wrong pickguard, wrong knobs

2)   Headstock of "Fender Jazz" bass counterfeit (replacement tuner)

3)   Forgery of Fender Jazz bass - has body based on some Korean-made Dean models

4)   Headstock of Fender Jazz bass forgery - note sloppy, one-color logo

5)   Counterfeit Fender Stratocaster

6)   Close-up of counterfeit Fender Stratocaster headstock; (real Fender Stratocasters do not have a truss rod cover like this one)

1) Cheap forgery with a metallic "Fender" logo stuck on headstock

2) Close-up of phony metallic "Fender" logo stuck on headstock of forgery

3) "Fender Stratocaster" counterfeit bass - the body actually looks more like a Music Man brand bass
(there is no such thing as a Stratocaster bass)

4) Headstock of phony "Fender Stratocaster" bass

5) Counterfeit Fender "Stratocaster" bass

6) Headstock of phony Fender "Stratocaster Bass" logo is gold outline only (real Fender logos are two-tone)

1)   Gibson bass forgery: looks nothing like a real Gibson resembles a Fender or G & L bass

2)   Close-up of Gibson bass forgery headstock; two-color logo with "sickle"-shaped 'G'

3)   Gibson forgery

4)   Close-up of headstock of Gibson forgery; letters of name are not in script, logo has gold border (real Gibsons have one-color logo)

5)   Counterfeit of Gibson EB-3 bass

6)   Close-up of headstock of Gibson EB-3 counterfeit---hints that this is a phony include a single white logo and crummy tuners

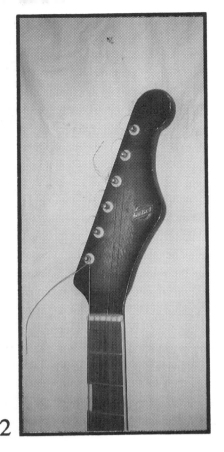

1   1

2

1)   Home-made Gretsch forgery; a cheap import,
probably made by Teisco Del Rey, that has a
polystyrene plastic Gretsch logo stuck on the
headstock.   The logo is probably from a real Gretsch
amplifier
2)   Close-up of Gretsch logo on headstock of forgery

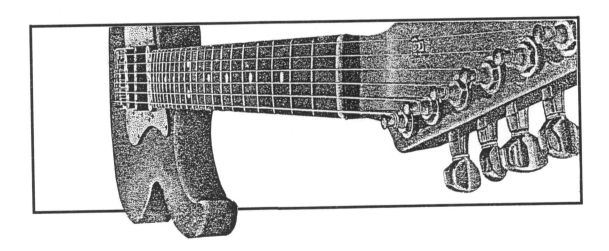

OUTRO

Malc perused the rough draft of this book, and pronounced the manuscript to be "the Gibson Melody Maker or the Fender Mustang of guitar books".

You know, he's not too far from right. It is my hope that anyone who's read this book will consider it to have been somewhat of an **introductory** course; i.e., "just the basics".

Obviously, if I had to recommend any further reading, I'd immediately cite each and every book listed in the Bibliography, but in particular I'd encourage the reader to check into Tom Wheeler's two books, The Guitar Book and American Guitars. The Guitar Book is, for all intents and purposes, an "encyclopedia" of information concerning the construction of guitars, playing and care of instruments. If The Guitar Book is an "encyclopedia", then American Guitars is the "Bible" for guitar collectors. In all honesty, some of the brands cited in this book's chapter on American brand names were only found in American Guitars.

Other books that were about to be released or that were "in the works" as this handbook was being prepared included ones on Gretsch instruments (by Jay Scott), Epiphone (by L.B. Fred), the Gibson Super 400 (by Dr. Tom Van Hoose), National (by Bob Brozman, who is a noted performer on National brand resonator guitars' his book should concentrate more on this unique type of instrument), and Fifties Kay guitars (Jay Scott again).

Vintage authorities George Gruhn and Walter Carter have recently released Gruhn's Guide to Vintage Guitars, which contains very detailed information about dozens of brands. As of this writing, a follow-up picture book from Gruhn and Carter is also being planned. A recent guitar book that concentrates on picture of instruments from around the world is Tony Bacon's The Ultimate Guitar Book.

In late 1991, Frenchman Andre Duchossoir released a book on Fender Telecaster guitars that is every bit as detailed as his book on Stratocasters. So it goes without saying that more and more information on classic U.S. guitars is becoming available, and any or all of the preceding sources would help increase an individual's guitar knowledge.

Another book that is reported to be in the works (by Centerstream Publications) is a large "anthology" of serial numbers for major U.S. manufacturers. Serial numbers on instruments are helpful in identifying the approximate year of a particular guitar or bass, but sometimes serial numbers do not follow an absolutely accurate pattern. For example, Gibson's serial number system from the early Seventies **makes no sense whatsoever** to most guitar buffs. Many of the books listed in the bibliography contain serial number lists, but the upcoming serial number anthology should be considered as well. Just remember that a serial number alone will not tell much about an instrument's history other than the approximate (if not accurate) year that it was made.

Probably the best move a pawn shop or owner can make regarding information on classic American guitars and basses is to inquire to either a guitar enthusiast/collector or vintage shop for a qualified opinion about the desirability and/or value of an instrument you might own, particularly if you are considering selling it. It pays off for everyone whenever information about American instruments is kept accurate and honest.

And if you **do** opt to sell your guitar or bass, please sell it to someone who has a genuine interest in classic American instruments (or if sold to a vintage shop, the shop would most likely sell it to someone who will appreciate the instrument for what it is and "give it a good home"). As stated earlier, financial transactions (whether through vintage shops or private sales) would hopefully be done in a manner so that everyone would be satisfied.

There are many fine luthiers building extraordinarily fine instruments in the U.S. these days; likewise, brands such as Peavey demonstrate that American companies can still build a quality, reasonably-priced guitar or bass. However, the days of dominance for U.S. guitar companies are probably gone forever. Accordingly, instruments from the "glory days" of American guitar manufacturing need to sought out, cleaned up and treated with respect.

After all, who knows what someone might have gathering dust in a closet or under a bed???

BIBLIOGRAPHY:

BOOKS:

Achard, Ken. The Fender Guitar (Westport, Connecticut: The Bold Strummer, Ltd. 1990) (First published in 1977 by Musical New Services Ltd, London. A Guitar Magazine project) Re-Issue

Bishop, Ian C. The Gibson Guitar from 1950 (London, England: Musical New Services, Ltd., 1977. A Guitar Magazine project)

Bishop, Ian C. The Gibson Guitar from 1950, Vol. 2 (Westport, Connecticut: The Bold Strummer, Ltd. 1990) (First published by Musical New Services, Ltd, London in 1979. A Guitar Magazine project) Re-Issue

Blackburn, Bill. Old Guitar Mania (Fullerton, California: Centerstream Publishing 1992)

Blasquiz, Klaus. The Fender Bass (Mediapresse 1990)

Brosnac, Donald (Editor). Guitar History, Volume 1: Guitars Made By The Fender Company (Westport, Connecticut: The Bold Strummer, Ltd. 1983, 1986)

Brozman, Bob. The National Guitar (Fullerton, California: Centerstream Publishing 1992)

Bulli, John. Guitar History, Volume 2: Gibson SG (Westport, Connecticut: The Bold Strummer, Ltd. 1989)

Crocker, Dave; Brinkman, John; and Briggs, Larry. Guitars, Guitars, Guitars (Neosho, Missouri: All American Music Publishers 1988)

Day, Paul. The Burns Book (London, England: PP Publishing 1979)

Duchossoir, A.T. Gibson Electrics, Vol. 1 (Milwaukee, Wisconsin: Hal Leonard Publishing Corporation 1981)

Duchossoir, A.R. Guitar Identification Fender-Gibson-Gretsch-Martin (Milwaukee, Wisconsin: Hal Leonard Publishing Corporation 1983)

Duchossoir, A.R. The Fender Stratocaster 1954-1984 (Milwaukee, Wisconsin: Hal Leonard Publishing Corporation 1983)

Duchossoir, A.R. The Fender Stratocaster (revised edition) (Milwaukee, Wisconsin: Hal Leonard Publishing Corporation 1988)

Evans, Tom and Mary Anne. Guitars: from the Renaissance to Rock (Facts on File Publishing)

Hartman, Robert Carl. Guitars and Mandolins in America, featuring the Larsons' Creations (revised edition) (Hoffman Estates, Illinois: Maurer & Co. Printing and Publication 1988)

Iwanade, Yasuhiko, The History of the Fender Stratocaster (Fullerton, California Centerstream Publishing 1991)

Longworth, Mike. Martin Guitars, A History (third edition) (Minisink Hills, Pennsylvania: 4 Maples Press Inc. 1988)

Schmidt, Paul. Acquired of the Angels: The Lives and Works of John D'Angelico and James D'Aquisto (Scarecrow Press)

Scott, Jay. The Guitars of Fred Gretsch (Fullerton, California: Centerstream Publishing 1991)

Smith, Richard R. The History of Rickenbacker Guitars (Fullerton, California: Centerstream Publishing 1987)

Tsumura, Akira. Guitars: The Tsumura Collection (Tokyo, Japan and New York, New York: Kodansha International, Ltd. 1987)

Wheeler, Tom. The Guitar Book (New York, New York: Harper & Row Publishers, Inc. 1974)

Wheeler, Tom. American Guitars (New York, New York: Harper & Row Publishers, Inc. 1982)

Wilcott and Ball. The Musical Instrument Collector (Bold Strummer)

CATALOGS, BROCHURES, POSTERS and CATALOG RE-PRINTS (by year):

Adamas-1982
Alembic-1982, 1985
Carvin-1978, 1983, 1986
Fender-1964, 1967, 1970, 1972, 1978, 1979, 1982, 1983, 1984,1989, 1990
G & L-1990
Gibson-1965, 1966, 1970, 1979, 1983, 1987, 1988, 1989, 1990
Hamer-1982, 1988, 1989
Harmony-1958, 1961
Kramer-1979, 1983, 1987, 1990
Kustom-1967 (?)
Mosrite-1972
Music Man-1980
Peavey-1982, 1989
Rickenbacker-1975, 1984, 1985, 1986
Robin-1988
Sears catalog reprints-Fall 1946, Fall 1958, Spring 1960, Fall 1960,.
Spring 1961, Fall 1961
Ken Smith-1981
Valco-1968

(As stated in the "Intro", much of the information was furnished by individuals and companies listed at the beginning of the book; such information was obtained by phone calls and/or correspondence).

Other guitar books from CENTERSTREAM